World Economics Associati
BOOK SERIES

MW00475246

Economics, ideological orientation and democracy for sustainable development

2nd Edition

Peter Söderbaum

World Economics Association BOOK SERIES

Economics, ideological orientation and democracy for sustainable development, 2nd Edition
by Peter Söderbaum

Copyright © 2016, 2018 Peter Söderbaum

ISBN: 978-1-911156-38-3 (paperback)
       978-1-911156-37-6 (eBook, Mobi)
       978-1-911156-39-0 (eBook, PDF)

Published by World Economics Association, Bristol, UK
www.worldeconomicsassociation.org

The **World Economics Association (WEA)** was launched on May 16, 2011. Already over 13,000 economists and related scholars have joined. This phenomenal success has come about because the WEA fills a huge gap in the international community of economists – the absence of a professional organization which is truly international and pluralist.

The World Economics Association seeks to increase the relevance, breadth and depth of economic thought. Its key qualities are worldwide membership and governance, and inclusiveness with respect to: (a) the variety of theoretical perspectives; (b) the range of human activities and issues which fall within the broad domain of economics; and (c) the study of the world's diverse economies.

The Association's activities centre on the development, promotion and diffusion of economic research and knowledge and on illuminating their social character.

The WEA publishes books, three open-access journals (*Economic Thought, World Social and Economic Review* and *Real-World Economics Review*), a bi-monthly newsletter, blogs, holds global online conferences, runs a textbook commentaries project and an eBook library.

CONTENTS

PREFACE

There are a number of schools of thought in economics but economics education is largely limited to one perspective – so called "neoclassical theory". When education is concerned, reference can be made to a monopoly situation for neoclassical economics. This standardization of economics education nationally and globally has its advantages, for example, in the sense that economists largely understand each other and speak the same language.

But this monopoly and standardization process is not without problems. Neoclassical theory may be useful for some purposes and problems, but not all problems. Reference to one single, standard perspective is like "putting all eggs in one basket". If the conceptual framework and language of neoclassical theory, with all its assumptions, is not so constructive in relation to some issues, then we have reason to look for other theoretical perspectives or paradigms.

Economics is important as the language of governance and management of resources at various levels from the individual and groups to organizations, local communities, nations and even the global society. As with other social sciences, the assumptions and conceptual framework of economics is not just a matter of science but at the same time, values and ideology. Limiting economics education to one single paradigm therefore means that (often publicly financed) university departments of economics get a political and ideological role not compatible with normal ideas of democracy. A first step here is to open the door for some degree of pluralism in economics. The important thing is to show that there are alternatives to neoclassical theory. One among such alternatives is presented in this book.

While there are some reasons for optimism these days, for example student associations who call for pluralism in economics education (www.isipe.net/open-letter) and professional associations like WEA (World Economics Association), it appears as if good arguments are not enough to open up economics for pluralism. When international trade is concerned neoclassical economists preach that "free trade" is good while "protectionism" is bad but when it comes to their own theory, "protectionism" has been the main strategy. This suggests that political intervention from outside, with reference to the failures of neoclassical theory and misconduct in relation to normal ideas of democracy, is very much needed.

In the present book, sustainability issues like climate change, biodiversity loss, and pollution will be emphasized. Something can certainly be achieved within the scope of neoclassical theory, method and policy proposals (environmental taxes or charges and financial support to activities expected to be sustainable, for example) but our chances of dealing constructively with these challenges will presumably increase if economists open the door for competing paradigms. It can safely be argued that neoclassical theory, so far, has not succeeded in dealing with these problems.

Uppsala 2016-02-19
Peter Söderbaum

In the present extended version of the book Chapters 6, 7 and 8 are new. In Chapter 6 the actor-network perspective is further elaborated as is the potential role of economics students. Chapter 7 focuses on "ideology" and "ideological orientation" as essential concepts in economic analysis. Sustainable development, for instance, can be understood as an ideological orientation that differs from neoliberalism the latter with its emphasis on GDP-growth and monetary profits in business. In Chapter 8 expectations on various actor categories in relation to sustainable development are discussed. In an Appendix (previous Chapter 6 in the earlier version) some experiences of the author as actor are indicated. Professors of economics are not neutral actors.

Uppsala 2017-11-16
Peter Söderbaum

ACKNOWLEDGEMENTS

No one is totally independent of others when writing a book. I have in particular benefited from dialogue with the following "political economic persons" (to use the vocabulary in the present book): Jan Bengtsson, ecology, Swedish University or Agricultural Sciences, SLU, Uppsala, Kjell-Åke Brorsson, ecological economics, Mälardalen University, Västerås, Judy Brown, accounting, Victoria University of Wellington, New Zealand, Judith Dellheim, Rosa Luxemburg Foundation, Berlin, Malgorzata Dereniowska, ethics and philosophy, Poland, Fatima Ferraz, FADO Consulting, Ltd., Johannesburg, South Africa, Edward Fullbrook, executive director, World Economics Association, Håkan Håkansson, business management, BI, Norwegian Business School, Ove Jakobsen, Center for Ecological Economics and Ethics, Bodö School of Economics, Norway, Bo Kjellén, diplomat in environmental affairs, Uppsala, Eva Kras, Canadian Society for Ecological Economics, Cecilia Mark-Herbert, economic sciences, SLU, Uppsala, Masayuki Omori, institutional ecological economics, Meiji University, Tokyo, Neil Powell, Center for Sustainable Development, Uppsala University, Anatol Pikas, educational science, Uppsala University, Jack Reardon, Hamline University, Minnesota, Ali Douai, ecological economics, University of Nice, France, Stanislav Shmelev, Environment Europe, Oxford, Cecilia Tortajada, water management, National University of Singapore, Alexandra Waluszewski, organization theory, Department of Economic History, Uppsala University, Ulf Johanson, organization theory, Uppsala. I am also indebted to students for example at the international Master program in Sustainable Development, a collaborative project with Uppsala University and SLU, Swedish University of Agricultural Sciences.

Dialogue with these persons does not necessarily mean that they share my opinions or analysis. The usual disclaimers apply. Thank you also to Mälardalen University and its Academy of Business, Society and Engineering under the leadership of Thomas Wahl and Ulf R. Andersson and to Saywan Jamal and Rolf Andberger for offering assistance so much needed. I am not always friend with my computers. Finally, I want to express my thanks to Kyla Rushman who edited the book.

CHAPTER 1
The illusion of a value-free economics

Mainstream neoclassical theory is built upon specific ideas of good science. The main belief appears to be that economics is not much different from physics. What is good physics research and analysis then should apply also for economics. Along this line of reasoning, neoclassical economists have argued that if there are Nobel Prizes in physics and other natural sciences, then there should be a Nobel Prize also in economics. Since Alfred Nobel did not point to economics in his will, the Swedish Academy of Sciences has been reluctant to make the economics prize comparable with the original set of prizes. As we all know the economics award is correctly named "the Bank of Sweden Prize in Economic Sciences in Memory of Alfred Nobel".

In physics there is an emphasis on explanation by testing hypotheses and making experiments of a controlled kind. The scholar is an outside observer and value-neutrality is the norm. In social sciences, such as psychology and economics, the testing of hypotheses is not so easily done for different reasons. But those who believe in these ideas of good science can of course continue to emphasize experimental evidence.

One of the "disturbing factors" when it comes to social science is that value or ideological issues are involved and, I would say, unavoidable. (This may be so but to a lesser extent also in physics, chemistry and medicine.) The Bank of Sweden Economics Prize then gets a more complex role of not only rewarding scientific achievements but also having an ideological and political impact upon individuals and society. With few exceptions, the tendency has been to reward scholars who contribute to further strengthening not only mainstream neoclassical theory but also the present market-oriented political-economic system. In a recent book *The Nobel Factor. The Prize in Economics, Social Democracy, and the Market Turn* (2016) Avner Offer and Gabriel Söderberg discuss the ideological impact of the Prize in Swedish Politics. The Bank of Sweden Prize should not be presented as a purely scientific award. It is at the same time part of an ongoing ideological and political debate. To the extent that my "hypothesis" about the winners of the Bank of Sweden Prize is correct, those responsible for this award have a problem in relation to normal ideals of democracy.

Another side of this "physics envy" tendency of neoclassical economics is a preference for a mathematical language. Only that which can be expressed in numerical terms counts. Monetary impacts are at the heart of neoclassical analysis and prices, in monetary terms, are used to make different impacts comparable and exchangeable. But this "monetary reductionism" and other kinds of quantification have its "price". Again mathematics has its role and advantages but obsession with mathematical presentation in social sciences and humanities will bring us further away from the real world of actors with their specific languages. As is the case with other languages, mathematics has its potential but also limitations.

Finally, neoclassical economists have largely accepted the idea of "paradigm-shift" originally suggested by Thomas Kuhn (1970) as applicable to the development of natural sciences. It is suggested that only one model or paradigm can be true in relation to a particular category of phenomena. Either paradigm A or paradigm B is correct in the sense of offering the best explanation. At a particular time, paradigm A is believed to offer the best understanding of the phenomena under study. When anomalies appear and some other paradigm B claims to offer a better explanation, a paradigm-shift may occur.

Thinking in terms of one paradigm at a time becomes an additional element of the protectionist tendency among neoclassical economists. The alternative here is to think in terms of "paradigm co-existence" (Söderbaum, 2000, pp. 29-31). Even in natural sciences, a category of phenomena, such as light, can be explained in more ways than one. When bringing in value-issues as in social sciences, the reasons to open the door for more than one perspective multiply. Truth – to the extent that reference to truth is made – becomes a matter of the theoretical *and* ideological perspective chosen. And we are back to the assertion that a single theoretical and ideological perspective need not exclude other perspectives. Actually, as we will see, ideology is involved even in the very way that economics is defined and understood.

Gunnar Myrdal on values in economics

I have already expressed criticism against the Bank of Sweden Economics Prize but I should also admit that there are exceptions. Especially in the early period, some broad-minded and interdisciplinary oriented economists were awarded. One case in point is Gunnar Myrdal. He drew attention to the need for a serious discussion of how values influence our work as economists:

> "Valuations are always with us. Disinterested research there has never been and can never be. Prior to answers there must be questions. There can be no view except from a viewpoint. In the questions raised and the viewpoint chosen, valuations are implied.
>
> Our valuations determine our approaches to a problem, the definition of our concepts, the choice of models, the selection of observations, the presentations of our conclusions – in fact the whole pursuit of a study from beginning to end" (Myrdal 1978, pp.778-779).

Myrdal refers to "valuations" rather than "values" perhaps as a way of distinguishing "valuations" from values in a monetary sense that plays such a role in mainstream economics. I will primarily refer to "ideology" and "ideological orientation" as will be explained later. For the moment let us emphasize Myrdal's argument that value issues need to be openly discussed. In a democratic society we do not need to share the same values but we should tolerate the values of others (as long as they do not contradict democracy itself). And we should respect the fact that a person's value or ideological orientation may be changing over time and is normally challenged in a political ongoing process that hopefully is leading to a better society.

Myrdal exaggerates a bit perhaps when suggesting that valuations "determine" our approaches to a problem, the choice of models, the selection of observations, etc. Other factors are certainly involved as well. In any case, one implication of Myrdal's arguments is that economics cannot be regarded as based on scientific criteria alone. If values or ideology is involved then our ideas of democracy also become important. In addition to Myrdal's general references to definitions, models and methods we need to discuss the kind of ideas that are relevant in economic studies. How do schools of thought in economics differ?

Tanja von Egan-Krieger on similarities and differences between schools of thought in economics

In her book *Die Illusion wertfreier Ökonomie. Eine Untersuchung der Normativität heterodoxer Theorien* (2014), Tanja von Egan-Krieger compares different schools of thought in economics, mainstream neoclassical economics included. Among heterodox schools, she focuses on feminist economics, institutional economics and ecological economics. Already the terminology used for these schools suggest that ideology is involved; feminist economists emphasize the role of women in contemporary society and economy (unpaid work etc.), institutional economists argue that institutional and evolutionary perspectives are largely neglected in mainstream economics and ecological economists – at least some of us – believe that the present environmental and sustainability crisis calls for fundamental changes in economics at the level of paradigms.

But von Egan-Krieger does not focus directly on the heterodox schools. She also presents and scrutinizes mainstream neoclassical theory and has understood that there is some (although limited) flexibility also within the neoclassical paradigm. It is possible to study feminist problems within the scope of the neoclassical theory. Neoclassical economists have similarly responded to the critique from institutional economists by somewhat opportunistically creating their own "new institutional economics" with "transaction costs" as a main concept. And as we all know there is a neoclassical environmental economics that claims to deal seriously with environmental problems. Allegiance to the neoclassical paradigm makes the analysis a bit constrained however.

The logic and scheme of presentation in the book then looks as follows. For each group of economists, von Egan-Krieger has selected authors and texts considered representative for the group:

- Mainstream neoclassical economics in relation to ethics
- Critical examination of neoclassical theory generally
- Critical examination of applications of neoclassical theory
    - "New home economics" (Becker, 1976, 1981)
    - "New institutional economics" (Williamson, 1975; North 1990)
    - Environmental economics (Wiemann, 1995, 1999; Hambicke, 1992, 2001)
- Critical examination of Feminist economics (Biesecker and Hofmeister, 2006; Biesecker and Kesting, 2003)
- Critical examination of Institutional economics (Tool, 2001; Hodgson, 1988, 2001)
- Critical examination of Ecological economics (Daly, 1996, 2007; Daly and Cobb, 1989; Daly and Farley, 2010; Söderbaum, 2000, 2008a)

It may be noted that "critical examination of" here stands for an attempt to evaluate the different contributions negatively as well as positively.

While the international dialogue about economics is largely limited to the English speaking world of UK and North America, one interesting feature of von Egan-Krieger's analysis is that she has chosen to also focus on studies from the German speaking world. Rather than studying the work by David Pearce (1989) among neoclassical environmental economists for example, she has chosen texts from two authors, Joachim Wiemann and Ulrich Hambicke, who publish in German.

It is not possible here to go into detail about Tanja von Egan-Krieger's arguments and analysis. Her book should make it clear however that there is no value-free or value-neutral economics and that there are alternatives to neoclassical theory. She has chosen to consider Feminist, Institutional and Ecological economics but there are additional possibilities as well, such as Post-Keynesian economics and Marxist economics. In the case of the latter school, no one can doubt that ideology is involved.

Economists who have invested their career in neoclassical theory may feel uncomfortable when hearing about alternatives to neoclassical theory. But considering the value or ideological aspects of economics such reactions are equal to being scared of democracy. In a democracy we are supposed to listen to different voices. Part of this uneasiness may furthermore have to do with the mentioned tendency that neoclassical economists look upon their discipline in "paradigm-shift" terms. But as part of our present "paradigm co-existence" perspective, neoclassical theory will still be considered among alternatives.

Does all this mean that we have to face an unlimited number of theoretical perspectives? No, but it is suggested that one should be open-minded rather than close one's eyes when an actor suggests that sustainability problems (or other problems) need to be approached at a paradigm level. There are differences between the schools as discussed by von Egan-Krieger but also similarities. There are even differences within each group of economists for example between Oliver Williamson and Douglass North in the "New institutionalist" category or between Herman Daly and myself as two ecological economists. A specific scholar may furthermore have sympathies with more than one school or paradigm. As an example my own identity is connected with Institutional as well as Ecological economics. I appreciate also some of the work done by feminist or social economists.

Economists as political actors in a democratic society

Rather than propagating ideas about economists as neutral professionals and observers, we have to admit that we are political actors in a democratic society. As actors in society we should observe normal imperatives of democracy as well as some traditional rules of good science.

Economists are of course not the only political actors. Individuals as citizens (and in other roles) and organizations should also be regarded as political actors in the economy. Democracy has to become an essential element of economics, even influencing the way economics is defined.

Another conclusion from this chapter is that economics cannot be limited to one single alleged true perspective. Textbooks in economics have to be rewritten to reflect a pluralist attitude with respect to paradigms and schools of thought.

CHAPTER 2

Redefining economics in relation to multidimensional thinking and democracy

If value or ideological issues are necessarily involved in economic analysis then this is also relevant for how economics is defined. Traditional ways of defining economics as "efficient management of scarce resources" emphasize certain values and ways of dealing with value issues. Some idea of "efficiency" is advocated which normally points to a special role for the monetary dimension. "Resources" tend to be looked upon in terms of prices and the monetary aspect. This focus on money is the starting point for analysis of optimality in terms of quantitative monetary calculation. At the societal level Cost-Benefit Analysis (CBA) and sometimes cost-efficiency analysis are proposed and this focus on the monetary dimension is equally valid for the micro level where monetary profits in business and monetary income of individuals play a major role. And, as we all know, for the total economy increase in Gross Domestic Product is looked upon as an essential monetary objective by many.

The relative importance of money and the monetary dimension should however be an open issue in a democratic society. Other perspectives and dimensions may be considered relevant. A more open definition of economics appears to be appropriate.

Redefining economics

If values and ideology are involved in defining economics, then there is a choice. Which values are relevant for studies and analysis at the societal level? Once more we can consult the works by Gunnar Myrdal. In his analysis of development issues in the United States (Myrdal, 1944), he used the constitution of the USA as his point of departure. The constitution of a country or nation expresses a kind of meta-ideology that all citizens are expected to agree about and follow. In countries like USA and Sweden, the constitution establishes fundamental ideas about governance, such as democracy and human rights. It is here suggested that "democracy" becomes an essential part of our understanding of economics.

To institutionalists, democracy appears as a "meta-institution" among institutional arrangements. This is true of Marc Tool's book *The Discretionary Economy* (2001). An institutional economist who emphasizes democracy in relation to environmental or sustainability issues and similarly argues that economics has to move closer to a view of individuals as actors understood in political terms with their opportunities for action and responsibilities is Peter Jakubowski. His book *Democratische Umweltpolitik* (1999) and article "Political Economic Person contra Homo oeconomicus – Mit PEP zu Mehr Nachhaltigkeit" (2000) are examples.

Myrdal was also open-minded in relation to interdisciplinary and multidimensional thinking (Myrdal, 1968). This is a second element that I want to bring into the definition of economics:

> "Economics is understood as multidimensional management of
> (limited) resources in a democratic society".

The role of various monetary and non-monetary dimensions for decision-making purposes then becomes an open issue to be considered, discussed and decided in a society that respects normal ideas of democracy.

It is here suggested that we as economists move some steps away from technocracy toward democracy. Experts in different fields of knowledge are certainly needed but relying exclusively on experts is not a wise strategy. Cost-Benefit Analysis (CBA), as previously mentioned, is an extremely technocratic approach where economists as experts are expected to identify correct values in market terms (prices) for social assessment of alternatives of choice. Why should one give priority to this specific market ideology in a society where many other ideological orientations are represented by politicians and citizens?

The reference to "multidimensional" management of resources in turn represents a questioning of what I consider as "monetary reductionism" of mainstream neoclassical economics. Our definition of economics implies that non-financial and non-monetary impacts are as "economic" as financial and monetary ones. When ecological economics or economics of sustainability is concerned, it is clear that a large number of non-monetary resources and dimensions are involved. In Sweden for example 16 sets of environmental objectives have been formulated. These are:

1. Reduced climate impact
2. Clean air
3. Natural acidification only
4. A non-toxic environment
5. A protective ozone layer
6. A safe radiation environment
7. Zero eutrophication
8. Flourishing lakes and streams
9. Good-quality groundwater
10. A balanced marine environment. Flourishing coastal
    areas and archipelagos
11. Thriving wetlands
12. Sustainable forests
13. A varied agricultural landscape
14. A magnificent mountain landscape
15. A good built environment
16. A rich diversity of plant and animal life

Source: http://www.miljomal.se/sv/Environmental-Objectives-Portal/)

For each one of these environmental objectives there are a number of indicators and to bring things together reference is made to a "generation goal" as follows:

> "The overall goal of environmental policy is to hand over to the next generation a society in which the major environmental problems have been solved, without increasing environmental and health problems outside Sweden's borders."

It is suggested here that impacts related to each one of the 16 indicator groups are "economic" impacts and as such should be considered in their own terms rather than being translated into monetary impacts. The same principle is relevant for other non-monetary impacts, such as health impacts on individuals. Each non-monetary impact category may have its own features. Inertia in physical terms is one possibility. Pollution of CO_2 is accumulated in the atmosphere and should not mechanically be traded against financial or other non-monetary impacts. When road-construction is concerned, the monetary price and outlay when compensating farmers (and others) for land needed may be precisely estimated but the "price" (what is lost) in non-monetary terms by transforming parts of land surface from agricultural land to asphalt surface is largely irreversible. Irreversibility suggests that costs cannot be estimated meaningfully in monetary terms. It may vary from zero up to infinity if one insists on monetary valuation which in turn suggests that the usual one-dimensional monetary calculation breaks down.

It is here argued that an analyst has to "illuminate" estimated non-monetary impacts separately from estimated monetary impacts. At the level of a municipality or nation one has to monitor the total changes in land surface used for different purposes connected with all projects of house building, road construction etc. as a matter of non-monetary "economic" resources.

Responsible for monitoring and follow-up of the 16 environmental goals is the Swedish Environmental Protection Agency. Deterioration continues for most environmental objectives but some progress is also reported (www.miljomal.se/sv/Environmental-Objectives-Portal/). The official existence of environmental objectives is an important step forward but the attention (and internalization) of these objectives appears still limited among politicians compared with GDP-growth, employment and financial budget considerations. This suggests that we are back to the issues of paradigm and ideology.

United Nations: from Millennium Development Goals to Sustainable Development Goals

It is not only in the case of Swedish environmental policy that a disaggregated philosophy and strategy is gaining ground. Since the year 2000, the United Nations with its related organizations and programmes has elaborated and monitored eight separate but related "Millennium Development Goals" (United Nations, 2015). These are:

- Eradicate extreme poverty and hunger
- Achieve universal primary education
- Promote gender equality and empower women
- Reduce child mortality
- Improve maternal health
- Combat HIV/AIDS, malaria and other diseases
- Ensure environmental sustainability
- Develop a global partnership for development.

The Millennium Development Goals focused on the situation in the so called "developing nations". From 1915, a new development agenda has been articulated and made legitimate through the United Nations. It applies to all countries and not a limited set of countries. It is understood that sustainable development is as much – if not more – a challenge for so called "developed" countries. 17 "Sustainable Development Goals" (SDGs) have been formulated and 169 indicators to measure progress (United Nations, 2015). Not unexpectedly there is some similarity to the eight Millennium Development Goals:

- End poverty in all its forms everywhere
- End hunger, achieve food security and improved nutrition and promote sustainable agriculture
- Ensure healthy lives and promote well-being for all at all ages
- Ensure inclusive and equitable quality education and promote lifelong learning opportunities for all
- Achieve gender equality and empower all women and girls
- Ensure availability and sustainable management of water and sanitation for all
- Ensure access to affordable, reliable, sustainable and modern energy for all
- Promote sustained, inclusive and sustainable economic growth, full and productive employment and decent work for all
- Build resilient infrastructure, promote inclusive and sustainable industrialization and foster innovation
- Reduce inequality within and among nations
- Make cities and human settlements inclusive, safe, resilient and sustainable
- Ensure sustainable consumption and production patterns
- Take urgent action to combat climate change and its impacts
- Conserve and sustainably use the oceans, seas and marine resources for sustainable development
- Protect, restore and promote sustainable use of terrestrial ecosystems, sustainably manage forests, combat desertification, and halt and reverse land degradation and halt biodiversity loss
- Promote peaceful and inclusive societies for sustainable development, provide access to justice for all and build effective, accountable and inclusive institutions at all levels
- Strengthen the means of implementation and revitalize the global partnership for sustainable development.

The previous Millennium Development Goals and the present Sustainable Development Goals both exemplify a movement away from the one-dimensional ideas of progress in terms of economic growth. Traditional objectives, such as GDP-growth and employment, are still there but GDP-growth should now be "sustainable" rather than unsustainable. It should also be observed that the mentioned traditional objectives are now part of a much broader view where no attempt is made to reduce all kinds of goals and impacts to one dimension. Complexity is seen as a fact of life rather than being assumed away. Economics is no longer understood in limited neoclassical terms. Actually, it is suggested here that each one of the 17 goals is understood as an "economic" goal. What happens to our resources in the form of forests, oceans and lakes is "economic" whether one is focusing on markets and trade or not.

As I understand it, the document with 17 SDGs is an important step forward in the views about economics advocated by the UN organization. As will be made clear later on, some studies supported by UN organizations have not yet adopted the more holistic view of economics. I am thinking of the role of UNEP in the TEEB-study of 2010.

It is here argued that this philosophy of disaggregation (i.e. keeping things separate) is as relevant for the micro level of individuals and organizations as for the national and global level. Decisions can be prepared in multidimensional profile terms rather than in one-dimensional monetary terms. This can be done in more ways than one but Positional Analysis is the approach advocated in this book (see Chapter 4). Accounting systems for organizations or firms need similarly to be opened up and reconsidered (Brown and Dillard, 2015).

Tensions between technocracy and democracy

We certainly need professionals with specific kinds of knowledge as experts. But we also need politicians that are well informed about options when making decisions and who are ready to take responsibility for their actions. Relying almost exclusively on experts (technicians) is here referred to as "technocracy". The aforementioned neoclassical Cost-Benefit Analysis is a good example of this. The analyst claims to know how to identify that option which represents the highest monetary profitability to society as a whole. Politicians are expected to accept these profitability estimates (or perhaps identify mistakes within the scope of the CBA rules of calculation). This suggests that politicians are hardly needed and that they, as well as other actors, should rely on CBA experts.

Criticism of this idea of correct prices in monetary terms is not new. Ezra Mishan, himself a textbook writer on neoclassical Cost-Benefit Analysis (1971) later argued that CBA is built upon an assumption that there is a consensus in society about the *why CBA cannot be used to evaluate environ. problems*

CBA way of valuing impacts. Since no such consensus can be expected, in particular in relation to environmental problems, CBA can no longer be used (Mishan, 1980).

Democracy on the other hand is about listening to many voices (rather than one voice). And the opinions expressed by politicians and other actors may differ with respect to understanding of the situation and also with respect to ideological orientation. These statements or narratives of politicians and other concerned actors have to be brought into analysis rather than excluded. The purpose when preparing decisions then becomes one of *illuminating* an issue for actors who differ with respect to situation and ideological orientation. As will be discussed later on, "ideological orientation" is a broader concept than interests connected with specific stakeholders.

According to the perspective presented here, the analyst has to accept some complexity by identifying and articulating a limited number of ideological orientations that appear relevant in the specific decision situation. Any conclusions that follow will then be conditional and tentative in relation to each ideological orientation considered. An ideological orientation that emphasizes markets in a neoclassical sense and economic growth in GDP-terms will presumably lead to a different ranking of alternatives considered than a specific interpretation of sustainable development as ideological orientation.

In this way the analyst becomes a more unpretentious actor who accepts our dictum that values and ideology is unavoidably involved and that the analyst herself is part of the political process. The information brought forward to politicians and other actors and the process of interaction itself should be judged against democratic criteria, for example "many-sidedness" with respect to ideological orientations and alternatives considered. If some ideological orientations and alternatives (for example, those that take environmental issues seriously) are systematically excluded, then this may be reason for criticism of the analysis carried out.

The kind of analysis indicated will stimulate further debate rather than point to one single optimal solution. Analysis is carried out in a way that strengthens democracy rather than weakens it.

A classification of economic approaches to decision making

Our argument so far suggests that there are different approaches to decision-making. A first distinction can be made between highly aggregated, one-dimensional approaches and highly disaggregated, multidimensional approaches and a second distinction between ethically/ideologically closed approaches and those that are open in the same respects. In this way we get four categories, "a", "b", "c" and "d" (Table 2.1). Neoclassical CBA clearly belongs to the highly aggregated, ethically/ideologically closed category "a". It is a technocratic approach with reliance on the authority of experts who claim neutrality by referring to the rules of CBA analysis.

Multiple-criteria analysis stands for disaggregated, ideologically more open approaches in category "d". Reference is made to "multiple-criteria decision making" (MCDM) or "multiple-criteria decision-analysis" (MCDA). This is based on a judgment that many problems are complex in the sense that it is not enough to use one criterion or objective function. Multiple criteria and multiple dimensions are judged relevant and there is a possible conflict between such criteria in the sense that the ranking of alternatives for different criteria differ.

In the same sense, Positional Analysis (PA) – that will be emphasized here – can be described as a multiple-criteria approach but differs from MCDA in other respects. MCDA tends to be seen a practical tool to prepare decisions and does not raise issues at the level of perspectives, such as paradigm in economics, ideology or institutional arrangements. Contrary to MCDA, PA is part of a different paradigm in economics and opens the door for different ideological orientations where democracy is taken seriously. MCDA rather tends to be turned into simple mathematics although that need not be the case.

Table 2.1 Categories of approaches to decision making.

	Ethically/ideologically closed	Ethically/ideologically open
Highly aggregated/ one-dimensional	"a"	"b"
Highly disaggregated/ multidimensional	"c"	"d"

Source: Söderbaum, 2000, p. 80.

Environmental Impact Statement (EIS) and Environmental Impact Assessment (EIA) belong to the same category "d" (although limited in scope to environmental impacts). As we have seen environmental performance is often a matter of multiple criteria and ranking on the basis of such criteria may differ. It should be observed that environmental impacts are regarded as economic impacts according to our definition of economics above.

Categories "b" and "c" are less important for our present purposes. It is possible to think of highly aggregated but ethically/ideologically open approaches (category "b") as sensitivity analysis in one-dimensional terms where prices other than those given by CBA rules of calculation are considered. This would still exemplify "monetary reductionism", however. Category "c" may stand for multidimensional analysis where specific objectives are formulated in each dimension for "acceptable" performance. Various kinds of standards connected with certification schemes may be behind such ideas of acceptability.

It is also possible to point to intermediate approaches, such as so called "cost-efficiency analysis" where the ambition is to find the alternative that minimizes monetary costs to achieve a specific level of environmental (or other non-monetary) performance. This kind of two-dimensional analysis certainly represents a step (although limited) in the right direction toward multi-dimensional more democratic approaches.

Economics of biodiversity as a case: UN actors still recommend traditional CBA

Neoclassical theory and method is largely formulated in quantitative mathematical terms. There is also a focus on markets and the monetary dimension. It is believed that markets that are free from intervention by the state lead to harmony and equilibrium. But also regulated markets where incentives are manipulated to influence the behavior of firms and consumers are elements of what can be described as the scientific and ideological orientation of neoclassical economists. This is manifested in analysis and CBA is an example of these beliefs and preferences.

A number of ecological economists have pointed to the limits and danger of one-dimensional monetary analysis in relation to environmental and other development issues. How can one attribute specific limited values to loss of specific species as part of biological diversity or to each unit of CO_2 emission expected to influence climate change? But judging from a recent study *The Economics of Ecosystems and Biodiversity: Ecological and Economics Foundations* (Kumar, ed. 2010) even some ecological economists give way to this temptation to reduce analysis to a monetary dimension. In this so called TEEB-study, different kinds of ecosystems and "ecosystem services" are identified and attempts are made to find out the monetary value of each kind of ecosystem service and then put them together as part of a "Total Economic Value" of each single project.

The chief architect behind this ambitious TEEB-study is Pavan Sukhdev, an economist connected with Deutsche Bank but also working for United Nation Environmental Programme (UNEP). In a preface of the main text he argues as follows: "It is a common dictum that 'you cannot manage what you cannot measure' (p. xxv). In his summary of the preface on 'Mainstreaming TEEB', Sukhdev refers to "the world's dominant economic and political model":

> "Valuations are a powerful 'feedback mechanism' for a society that has distanced itself from the biosphere upon which its very health and survival depends. Economic valuation, in particular, communicates the value of Nature to society in the language of the world's dominant economic and political model. Mainstreaming this thinking and bringing it to the attention of policy makers, administrators, businesses and citizens is the essence of the central purpose of TEEB" (p. xxvii).

The study ends up with a number of recommendations in specific reports for National and International Policy Makers, Regional and Local Policy Makers and for Business. There is no attempt to put various schools of thought against each other. The main idea seems to be to protect neoclassical economics as science and ideology and to support a development of the present political economic system which includes the "commodification" of ecosystems and nature. This can be thought of as a successful lobbyist operation by some actor categories – neoclassical economists included.

Pavan Sukhdev's arguments and position can exemplify what Clive Spash refers to as "New Environmental Pragmatism" (Spash, 2013). According to this view action is needed as soon as possible and we cannot wait for abstract and sophisticated theories but should rather adapt policy to what we understand as mainstream thinking among politicians and people more generally. If people have become used to money numbers, then science should also adapt to this. The possibility that mainstream thinking is part of the problems faced, is overlooked.

It should, however, be made clear that the main TEEB-study, with its 400 pages, is more multi-facetted than Sukhdev's preface. In places it is even contradictory. A large number of neoclassical and ecological economists contributed to the text, some of whom pointed to problems with the main strategy as expressed by the study leader. And some of us ecological economists who did not participate have offered our criticism to the TEEB-study in other places (Spash, 2011; Spash et al. 2015; Söderbaum, 2013, 2015).

CHAPTER 3
From economic man to political economic person

When attempting to socially construct some alternative to mainstream neoclassical economics, it is probably a good idea to start with a view of individuals as actors in the economy. I will here suggest that neoclassical Economic Man is replaced with Political Economic Person.

Economic Man assumptions can, however, be used as a point of departure for the articulation of a different view of individuals in the economy. Economic Man is related to a context which consists of, and is limited to, markets: markets for commodities, capital markets and labor markets. As we have seen, also the environment, for example ecosystem services, is "commodified" to fit into this picture.

"economic man"

Each individual as Economic Man expresses her values as "preferences" for commodities, the idea being that the individual as consumer chooses a particular combination of different commodities that maximizes her utility within the scope of her (monetary) budget constraint. Willingness to pay in monetary terms is the main idea of values and valuing. Preferences for commodities are thought of as being neutral in the sense that the neoclassical economist as analyst accepts all kinds of preferences. The neoclassical economist as scientist does not make distinctions between preferences that are good for society and those that are harmful to society. But the idea that such distinctions should be avoided is, in itself, a value commitment.

Those of us who are interested in the political debate about climate change and other environmental or development issues, sooner or later realize that values and ideology are involved. Some life-styles of individuals are more environmentally harmful than others. If one wishes to analyze environmental issues in a serious manner, it becomes relevant to distinguish between preferences and also design policies that encourage certain preferences and life-styles rather than others. To facilitate such distinctions between preferences, the concept of "ideological orientation" will be brought into the picture. It will be suggested that a political economic person is an individual as actor guided by her ideological orientation.

Options at the level of perspectives

Ideology plays a role in the contemporary political debate in countries such as Sweden, UK, Germany or the USA. In these countries, there are political parties who each articulate their ideological platform in attempts to attract citizens as voters and in framing laws and policies. In the countries mentioned, neoliberalism has played an important role and is still dominant in many circles. Neoliberalism is an extreme market ideology with privatization of previously public domains (health, social care, education etc.) and proposals for market solutions to all kind of problems. Progress in society is measured by economic growth in GDP-terms.

As I see it, neoclassical economic theory and analysis has played a major role in supporting neoliberalism and making it legitimate. Neoliberalism is built upon beliefs in markets and in firms maximizing profits as being efficient for society as a whole. It is admitted that there may be single externalities and "market failure" in some sense and some cases, but this represents a modification only of a generally positive view of markets being close to fundamentalism.

In Sweden for example, the Social Democratic Party is now in power, a party critical to neoliberalism, for example the privatization projects of the previous Conservative government, but cautious in attempts to reverse the process. Leading social democrats are eager not to position themselves too far from the conservative parties and the previous government. The Green Party, being part of the new government, seems to be content with compromise and small steps in what they see as the right direction. Only the Left party is ready to seriously counteract previous neoliberal policies in Sweden.

My attempt to characterize the situation in Sweden is certainly subjective as well as incomplete and is only one among many possibilities. But my point is that ideology plays an essential role in attempts to understand and deal with environmental and development issues.

Something has been achieved with environmental and development policies in the past. But it is also true that we have failed in relation to climate change, biological diversity and chemical pollution. We can deal with such problems one by one and hopefully make some progress with suboptimal solutions. But we also need to take a look at options at the level of perspectives. There may be "paradigm failure" and "ideology failure". As I see it, the close to monopoly position of neoclassical theory at university departments of economics has played a role in the lack of progress in relation to environmental and development issues. It is not realistic to expect one paradigm which has been dominant when things have gone wrong to solve problems on its own. The related dominant position of neoliberalism can similarly be understood as an ideology failure.

Our conclusion then is that reductionist approaches in terms of optimization is not enough. We also need to bring in options at the level of perspectives, such as paradigm in economics and ideology. As already indicated, my "hypothesis" in this part is that the dominance of neoclassical economics and neoliberalism in combination has been dysfunctional in relation to attempts to seriously deal with economic issues in the fields of environment and development.

We can also conclude that ideology matters at the level of collectivities, such as political parties. Our next step is to suggest that ideology plays a role also at the level of individuals and that the concept can be used in defining a "political economic person": "A political economic person is an individual and actor in the economy who is guided by her ideological orientation."

A note on "post-normal science"

In view of the challenges faced, it is perhaps not enough to discuss options with respect to economics paradigm and ideology. Also our ideas about good science may need to be reconsidered or expanded. At the first conference with the International Society for Ecological Economics (ISEE) in Washington D.C., Silvio Funtowicz and Jerome Ravetz (1991) argued that "normal science" was not enough to deal with the problems faced. As we have seen, neoclassical economists rely largely on positivism with the testing of hypotheses, experimental approach, quantitative modelling and analysis in search for optimal solutions. Funtovicz and Ravetz pointed to the complexity and fuzziness of problems and the limits to our knowledge. Uncertainty has to be taken seriously as well as "ignorance", the fact that some uncertainty is irreducible. Our knowledge is often tentative and fragmentary; impacts are sometimes better understood in qualitative and visual terms than quantitatively. Logically closed models do not tell the whole story. It is therefore a wise research policy to bring in issues of paradigm and ideology as previously discussed.

Fuzzy problems suggest another reason to depart from extreme technocracy. The economist should be less pretentious in analysis and conclusions. We need to accept some diversity in approach. Diversity among heterodox approaches, as presented for example in Tanja von Egan-Krieger's previously mentioned study (2014), should not be seen as a weakness – but rather strength. Where neoclassical economists tend to see standardization of the economics profession as ideal (with universities producing "economists as homogenous commodities"), the diversity idea suggests that there should be some room for heterogeneity, for example in terms of experiences, engagement, personality and ideological orientation. The existence of more than one school of thought in economics and varieties within each school should not only reluctantly be accepted. It will tell us about the maturity of economics as a science.

Political economic person assumptions

Few people would deny that money plays a role in our present political economic system and that the neoclassical model of consumer behavior is relevant in important ways. We all know that our monetary income or budget puts limits to what we can buy. But the neoclassical model is simplistic and should not exclude other models, for example those based on social psychology and other interdisciplinary approaches. In the early 1970s, I was teaching a course in marketing and consumer behavior at the Department of Business Economics, Uppsala University, using textbooks focusing on a conceptual framework from psychology and sociology (Howard, 1963; Engel et al., 1968). A seller of commodities needs to understand consumers reasonably well and then concepts such as motive, role, relationship, cognition, emotions, dissonance, identity etc. play a role. The development of habits and changes in behavior was discussed in terms of learning theory. At the same department of management science we learnt about Herbert Simon's ideas of satisficing (rather than optimizing) behavior in business (March and Simon, 1958). Later James March's discussed "appropriateness" in relation to decision-making (1994).

More recently, interest in "behavioral economics" has increased and even in relation to environmental policy (Beckenbach and Kahlenborn, eds, 2016). I have contributed as part of this book project (Söderbaum, 2016).

Our "political economic person" is understood in similar socio-psychological terms. Behavior is not limited to markets and the context of the individual is understood in broader terms than markets. We may refer to contexts that are socio-cultural, institutional, physical man-made and ecological. And these contexts are part of the economy, not outside it.

Values, ethics, and even ideology, play a role in human decision-making and behavior. The individual is regarded as an actor who moves in a multi-dimensional context that is changing over time. Some paths are open, others are closed. Behavior is assumed to be guided by values and ethical considerations, such as justice, but for different reasons we prefer to refer to an "ideological orientation". "Value" in economics tends to be connected with – and limited to – the monetary dimension and ethics often refers to relationships between two actors while our interest is as much in broader views of progress in society. But ethical considerations in the mentioned sense are certainly part of an actor's ideological orientation.

The concepts of ideology and ideological orientation

Historically, the word "ideology" has been used in different ways. For some, "ideology" stands for something negative attributed to others. In the US context one can even find publications addressing sustainability issues where the author declares that global cooperation that is "pragmatic and non-ideological" (Nolan, 2009, p. 7) is needed to overcome the present "wild capitalism". Reference has even been made to "the end of ideology" (Fukuyama, 1992). Fukuyama made the judgment that a specific market ideology, neoliberalism, had 'outcompeted' all ideological alternatives and that we therefore do not need to continue debates in ideological terms.

In this book "Ideology" is about means-ends relationships. "Ideology" is used as something that will always be with us. "We cannot step out of our ideological shoes". "The end of ideology is in principle never possible". Ideologies "help us to make sense of the world by providing a framework through which we act in the world" (MacKencie, 1994 p. 19 and p. 21).

Douglass North similarly points to ideologies as present at the level of individuals:

> "By ideology, I mean the subjective perceptions (models, theories) all people possess to explain the world around them. Whether at the microlevel of individual relationships or at the macrolevel of organized ideologies providing integrated explanations of the past and the present, such as communism and religions, the *theories* individuals construct are *colored* by normative views of how the

world should be organized" (emphasis in original, North, 1990, p. 23).

In positional terms "ideology" refers to where you are (initial position), where you want to go (future positions) and how to get there (strategy). "Ideological orientation" is a concept that can be connected with "post-normal science" as previously discussed. It does not exclude quantitative objectives but puts them as elements of larger visions in multi-dimensional terms that might also be qualitative and visual. The ideological orientation of a person refers to the immediate future as well as a long-term future. It may be narrow or broad in terms of considering other people; it may be fragmentary and conflictual or more coherent. Just as the context of the individual is changing, also the individual's ideological orientation is adapted to new situations. It is assumed that all individuals in their different roles and situations are guided by an ideological orientation and the content of this ideological orientation is something to be investigated in each case rather than taken as given.

While "ideology" is used frequently at the collective level, I suggest that this concept or rather "ideological orientation" can be used also at the level of individuals. If political parties or other social movements do their best to articulate ideological platforms, they do this to attract or get support from individuals. An individual can respond positively, negatively or not at all to the ideas of a specific social movement by referring to what is here seen as her ideological orientation.

Behavior is largely habitual but sometimes an individual as actor faces two or more options and decisions are made. This is looked upon as a "matching" process (Figure 3.1). On the one hand is the individual with her ideological orientation, on the other hand the individual's perception of expected impacts in multi-dimensional profile terms of each alternative considered. Sometimes there is a good fit, in other cases none of the alternatives is considered "appropriate". Decisions are often made even with an ideological orientation that is fragmentary and uncertain and with fragmentary knowledge about alternatives and their impacts. Thinking in terms of "matching" processes, test of compatibility, "appropriateness" and even "pattern recognition" is a way of approaching problems that may be "fuzzy". But the idea of "pattern recognition" is relevant also when objectives are expressed in more precise terms. A satellite can be programmed to identify certain patterns on land surface – for example military installations. The idea of pattern recognition is relevant also in more trivial situations, for example, an individual walking in a forest whose brain and perceptive capabilities recognize certain kinds of mushrooms as edible. I may also look for recurrent behavioral patterns of specific professionals, for example neoclassical economists. This way of thinking is gaining ground as indicated by the existence of an *International Journal of Pattern Recognition*.

Figure 3.1 Decision-making as a matching process

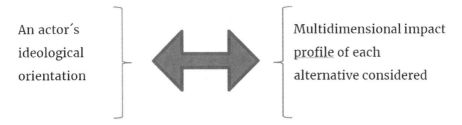

An actor's ideological orientation

Multidimensional impact profile of each alternative considered

Source: Söderbaum, 2000, pp. 40-41.

A main reason to use the term ideological orientation is however that I want to bring economics closer to political science and actual politics. Individuals are citizens in addition to consumers suggesting that economics has to be democratized (Söderbaum and Brown, 2010). Environmental and development issues involve ideological conflicts that have to be openly addressed rather than avoided. Climate change as an example is not only a matter of technicalities but also a paradigmatic and ideological issue. Referring to value-neutrality and systematically avoiding problems at the level of ideology is a dangerous strategy.

"Illuminate" rather than "solve"

Technocracy is characterized by expectations that experts are able to recommend solutions based on their scientific knowledge. Experts may certainly sometimes have such a role. But taking democracy seriously and respecting the complexity of problems faced tells us that we should listen to many voices and that a dialogue should be facilitated between interested parties and other concerned actors.

When decisions are taken in a political assembly at the local or national level, there are many actors and representatives of political parties who normally differ with respect to ideology or ideological orientation. The purpose of analysis then becomes one of "illuminating" the decision situation in relation to different ideological orientations rather than one single ideological orientation. Ideally, each decision maker, for example politician, should know what she or he is doing when voting for one alternative rather than another.

"Illuminate" is equal to "put light on" and suggests that visions and images are important in addition to numbers. Among economists Kenneth Boulding at an early stage wrote a book *The Image* (1956) where he pointed to new possibilities for economic theory and analysis but so far not with much influence.

The information basis presented to politicians or other decision-makers can normally be improved through further dialogue and studies. New alternatives may be presented and ideological orientations reconsidered.

CHAPTER 4
Ecological economics – a political perspective

Political economic person is just one element, albeit an important one, of an alternative economics for sustainable development. In Table 4.1 a comprehensive view of a conceptual framework for ecological economics is presented. But first some general comments that build on our previous alternative definition of economics:

Economics is always "political economics". "Values are always with us" as argued by Gunnar Myrdal. Values and ideological aspects of economic theory and analysis have to be dealt with openly. Marxist economists have attempted to monopolize the term "political economics". But all schools of thought in economics, neoclassical theory included, are varieties of political economics.

Normal imperatives of democracy are relevant for economics. Or, to put it differently: economics has to be democratized. Issues of the responsibility and accountability of various actors should be taken seriously. Mainstream neoclassical economics tends to foster technocracy. It can be noted that "democracy" is not part of the subject index of "Economics", a textbook by Gregory Mankiw and Mark Taylor (2014) for introductory economics courses that is used at many universities globally.

Ecosystems and natural resources are part of the economy, not outside it. In mainstream neoclassical textbooks, the economy is described as consisting of consumers, firms and the state (at the national level) that interact through different markets. It is admitted that the environment and third parties may be affected as the result of a market transaction. But so called "external impacts" are regarded as single impacts that can be internalized or compensated for. K. William Kapp among institutional economists argued that impacts on nature and ecosystems are ubiquitous and that many firms systematically reduce their monetary costs (and increase profits) by passing costs on to others and society at large, so called cost-shifting (Kapp, 1970, p. 18, 1971). And many of these costs are non-monetary in kind and carried over to future time periods. This is by Kapp referred to as the "principle of circular and cumulative causation" (Kapp, 2011, pp. 170-179).

Ideas about progress in society, in business or at the personal level have to be openly addressed and not be regarded as given. Economic growth in GDP terms and profits in business may be an essential part of an actor's ideological orientation or ideas about progress but other actors may have other priorities, for example some version of sustainable development or a Green economy. Economics as science cannot dictate "correct" priorities or goals for society or for business corporations.

Multidimensional monitoring systems need to be constructed and used at all levels from the global level through regional, national and local levels. Also individuals should be encouraged to think of their performance in multidimensional terms. It is no longer enough to focus on monetary impacts. Non-monetary impacts with their specific features (inertia, irreversibility, etc.) need to be made visible.

Just as paradigms do not completely exclude each other and may co-exist, the same holds for models of the individual, organization, market, etc. While each model may be judged by an actor as having both strengths and weaknesses in relation to specific purposes, it is also the case that one model of the individual (organization, market) may add to the understanding provided by another model.

In Table 4.1, a proposed conceptual framework for ecological economics is compared to the neoclassical perspective. Political economic person assumptions as alternative to Economic Man have already been touched upon.

Political economic organization assumptions

The only kind of organization dealt with in neoclassical microeconomics is the "firm" or business organization and the firm is expected to maximize monetary profits. Other objectives of firms than monetary ones, such as those connected with Corporate Social Responsibility (CSR) are not seriously considered. Organizations that cannot be described as firms, such as foundations, universities, churches, political parties and environmental organizations are considered as if they were firms or excluded from consideration.

Table 4.1 Conceptual framework for ecological economics.

	Neoclassical theory	Ecological economics
Individual	Economic Man	Political economic person (PEP)
Organization	Profit-maximizing firm	Political economic organization (PEO)
Market	Supply and demand as mechanistic forces	PEPs and PEOs as responsible market actors
Decision-making	Optimal solutions	Matching processes
Approaches to decision-making	Cost-Benefit Analysis (CBA)	Positional Analysis (PA)
Political economic system (institutional arrangements)	Assumed to be given	Changes all the time and should sometimes be challenged

The neoclassical "firm" is centralized in the sense that conflicts of interest within the firm are assumed away. Conflicts with actors outside the firm are understood in terms of competition with other firms. A first step towards considering more complex models is to identify different categories of stakeholders or interested parties in relation to a specific business or other organization (Rhenman, 1969; Freeman, 1984; Freeman et al., 2010). Examples of such stakeholders related to a business organization are suppliers, customers and consumers. These stakeholder categories differ in terms of interest and there are differences between actors within each of these categories. In addition to the "stakeholder model" there is a "network model" that focuses on relationships and dependencies between actors within an organization and in relation to actors in the outside world (Ford, 1990; Forsgren et al. 2005; Håkansson et al. 2009).

The "political economic organization model" adds further to the understanding offered by the neoclassical model, the stakeholder model and the network model. Individuals as actors within and outside the organization are characterized by their ideological orientation. Different opinions and conflicts within the organization and in relation to actors in the outside world become relevant to study. While there may be some tensions among actors related to an organization there are also normally some common interests that can be summarized in a "mission". This mission corresponds to ideological orientation at the level of individuals. The mission of a specific organization may be conflictual or coherent, one-dimensional or multi-dimensional.

Reference to political economic organization should also be understood as recognizing that organizations (and not exclusively business organizations) play a role in politics generally and for sustainable development, with specific responsibilities in a democratic society. Issues of Corporate Social Responsibility (CSR) or University Social Responsibility (USR), for that matter, are relevant as part of this perspective.

PEPs and PEOs as market actors

The neoclassical model of markets in terms of supply and demand is mechanistic. There is a focus on equilibrium between forces. Human beings on the supply and demand side are reduced to physical entities – like interacting molecules – as argued by Thorstein Veblen, an early institutional economist (Veblen, 1990. p. 73). Issues of power and ethics are not part of the picture.

In the neoclassical model, firms and customers/consumers are clearly separated from each other. This is challenged by the previously mentioned "network model" where interdependencies, trust and the possibility of cooperation between actors in different organizations is acknowledged. Rather than single companies competing with each other, networks or groups of corporations can be understood as the competing entities.

In the "political economic market model", political economic persons and political economic organizations are the market actors as sellers and buyers. Prices and other conditions of market exchange are negotiated and decided by humans. Issues of unequal power between parties in a transaction and the possibility of one exploiting the other may be considered relevant. Similarly issues of Corporate Social Responsibility (CSR), "fair trade" and "eco-labelling" and other certification schemes become relevant and visible as part of this model. Why should ethical considerations be viewed as being outside economic theory? Efficiency and rationality become largely a matter of an actor's ideological orientation.

Positional Analysis as alternative to neoclassical Cost-Benefit Analysis (CBA)

Neoclassical economists advocate a standardized approach to decisions at the level of society, so called Cost-Benefit Analysis (CBA). The approach is typically applied to proposed new infrastructure investments, such as roads, dams, public utilities and can be described as one-dimensional "trade-off" philosophy in monetary terms. All kinds of impacts are traded against each other at market prices dictated by the economist as expert, or rather the rules of valuation inherent to the method.

CBA exemplifies some of the critical points raised previously about neoclassical theory and method:

- Technocracy
- Monetary reductionism
- Ethical-ideological reductionism.

The purpose of CBA is to "solve" a problem, as previously discussed, by pointing to the best or "optimal" option through calculation in monetary terms. A discount rate is applied to deal with future impacts in the attempt to find a "present value" for each option considered.

Positional Analysis as alternative to CBA represents a move in the opposite direction:

- Democracy rather than technocracy
- Multidimensional analysis rather than monetary reductionism
- Analysis that is ethically/ideologically open rather than closed.

CBA is built on the assumption that there is a consensus in society about how alternatives can be evaluated in specific market terms. The Positional Analysis (PA) approach, on the other hand, is built upon the idea that no consensus about values or ideology can be assumed. In a democracy more than one ideological orientation is normally represented. The analyst should therefore identify three or four ideological orientations that appear relevant to politicians and other actors related to an issue. Conclusions, for example in the form of ranking alternatives, will then be conditional in relation to each ideological orientation considered.

The purpose of analysis is to "illuminate" an issue rather than solve it in any final terms. Each decision-maker should be well informed and know what she/he is doing when opting for one alternative or another. The move from one-dimensional monetary analysis to multidimensional analysis means that one has to deal with each impact on its own terms. While CBA is based on assumptions of extreme transformation – all kinds of impacts can meaningfully be interpreted in monetary terms – the PA-analyst respects differences in kind of impacts and tries to illuminate issues of inertia (lock-in effects, irreversibility, path-dependence) and of equality in ways that are understood by politicians and other decision-makers.

I will not go into details about Positional Analysis here. For a broad description and discussion of the approach see Brown et al., 2017 "Positional Analysis for Sustainable Development". The name of the approach needs however some clarification. In Table 4.2, a distinction is made between monetary and non-monetary variables in economic analysis and another distinction between flows and positions. A flow refers to a period of time whereas a position refers to a point in time. "Position" is equivalent to "state" or "stock". The reason for choosing the word "position" is that it appears more useful in relation to the some kinds of dimensions that may be relevant in impact studies. As an example one may refer to "social position" rather than "social state" or "social stock". "Power position" is another example.

Table 4.2 Categories of indicators or impacts in economic analysis.

	Flow (referring to period of time)	Position (referring to point in time)
Monetary	"e"	"f"
Non-monetary	"g"	"h"

Source: Söderbaum, 2000, p. 62.

In Table 4.2 category "e" impacts or indicators are exemplified by GDP, Gross Domestic Product. It is clearly a monetary variable that refers to a period of time, normally a year. The turnover of a company per year and the income of a person per month (or year) are other examples of monetary flows. The balance sheet of a company or other organization with assets and liabilities (or of an individual) similarly tells us about financial positions (category "f") since these numbers refer to the situation at a specific point in time.

On the non-monetary side, environmental impacts are normally described in terms of flows and positions (Cf. categories "g" and "h"). Pollution of CO_2, for example, is a flow that influences the position or state of carbon in the atmosphere and at other places. The size of land-use changes in a municipality between two points in time t_1 and t_2 influences the end position with respect to land-use at t_2 etc.

Figure 4.1 Decision tree in positional terms

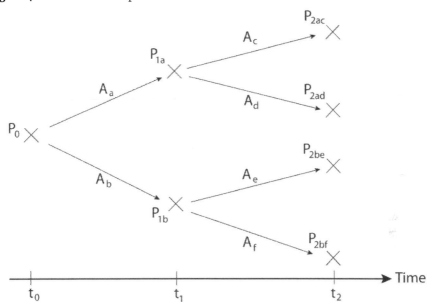

Source: Söderbaum 2000, p. 94.

The categories in Table 4.2 are not mutually exclusive. In a study all four kinds of indicators may be needed. Estimates of flows are often needed to estimate changes in positions (states) etc. But as the name of the approach suggests, "positional thinking" is an important element in "Positional Analysis". This can be illustrated with a specific kind of decision trees (Figure 4.1). P_0 stands for the initial position of a specific object of description at time t_0. Two options A_a and A_b are assumed to be available at t_0. One is to move to position P_{1a} at t_1 and another to move to position P_{1b} at the same future point in time t_1. At t_1 the options for further moves will differ between P_{1a} and P_{1b} and depend on the first move.

The logic is much like the logic in a game of chess. The first move by a player will condition further moves. Decision-making becomes a multiple-step process where each move will make options expand and contract in specific ways. In chess, player K is more or less uncertain about the plans of player L and therefore has to think in multiple steps and consider more than one strategy. A game of chess ends in a particular way. Only one player will win or there may be a draw. The path from beginning to end of the game can be described clearly in positional terms. A specific series of positions among all possibilities for the two players has led to the end of the game.

Moving now to decision-making in relation to physical infrastructure, such as dams, roads or housing, positional thinking means that changes in future options – by choosing one alternative rather than another – can be considered among consequences. Some actors may make a proposal that a park in a city is exploited for housing purposes. This would lead directly to a number of individuals and families getting flats for living purposes. But the exploitation is largely an irreversible land-use change. Such irreversible non-monetary changes in positions and their implications need to be illuminated for decision-makers before a decision is taken.

This is common sense, one may object. Yes, but at issue is how such irreversible changes are considered in traditional approaches to decision-making, such as CBA. They tend to disappear since no meaningful monetary value can be attributed to such impacts.

Actually, the impacts of choosing one alternative at time t_0 can be described as a series of non-monetary (and monetary) positions connected with alternative paths in a decision tree. In Figure 4.1 (which is admittedly simplified) there are four alternative paths:

$$P_0 \longrightarrow P_{1a} \longrightarrow P_{2ac}$$
$$P_0 \longrightarrow P_{1a} \longrightarrow P_{2ad}$$
$$P_0 \longrightarrow P_{1b} \longrightarrow P_{2be}$$
$$P_0 \longrightarrow P_{1b} \longrightarrow P_{2bf}$$

P_0 stands for position at time t_0, P_{1a} for position at time t_1 in the case that alternative A_a is chosen at t_0 and P_{2ac} for position at time t_2 in the case that alternative A_a is chosen at t_0 and alternative A_c at t_1. But three other series of positions with their implications are considered at t_0.

When compared with traditional decision-trees in game theory, there is no final "pay-off" at the end of each path through the decision-tree. Decision-making is rather seen as a never ending process where each new position is a starting point for further moves.

Positional thinking calls into question the whole idea that future consequences of a decision can meaningfully be summarized and reduced into one numerical number, such as a "present value" in monetary terms. Various aspects of inertia and how it influences the future at different points in time need to be made visible. Will there be "commitments" with specific actors involved that limit options or moves later on? Is it reasonable to speak of "lock-in effects" or "path dependence"? Are some positional changes irreversible?

Positional changes can be illuminated not only in relation to monetary and physical/environmental changes. In the first study with PA (1973), a list of potentially relevant dimensions was given:

- Psychological dimensions
- Dimensions in relation to information and knowledge
- Social dimensions
- Ethical dimensions
- Legal and juridical dimensions
- Aesthetic dimensions
- Physical dimensions
- Biological dimensions
- Chemical dimensions
- Ecological dimensions
- Physical-technical dimensions
- Spatial dimensions
- Historical dimensions
- Monetary dimensions (Söderbaum, 1973, pp. 64-66).

The list can certainly be extended or presented in other ways. Positional thinking is relevant for example concerning learning and efforts to improve knowledge positions or stocks of knowledge. Or, we can point to the trivial example of a person walking, starting in a particular geographical and other position and how it changes over time. Actually, one example of positional thinking familiar to many these days is GPS, Global Positioning System, "a satellite navigation system used to determine the ground position of an object" or in other words: "a radio system that uses signals from satellites to tell you where you are and to give you direction to other places." Positional thinking in geographical terms is certainly of importance but a GPS-analogy can (much like the chess analogy) be used when extending positional thinking to different kinds of dimensions. Our psychic pleasures may be based on series of positions rather than the commodities that we buy in real or imagined markets. Or, can these ways of approaching welfare be combined in fruitful ways?

"Positional thinking" is not the only part of PA. "Systems thinking" is another part. At an early stage the analyst tries to identify those systems (of different kinds and with different spatial extensions) that are differently affected depending upon alternative chosen. Another potential part of PA is a kind of conflict analysis where the analyst tries to identify what kind of activities of individuals or organizations that are differently affected depending upon alternative chosen in the specific decision situation. For each activity identified, a goal direction can be assumed (less noise, shorter distance to work, more sales etc.) which permits a ranking of alternatives. A specific alternative may then be judged as good for some activities but normally not for all purposes (see Söderbaum, 2000, pp. 102-103).

Positional analysis is an attempt to face many aspects of complexity of a decision situation. But there are of course practical limits to what can be done. To make analysis tractable, it may be appropriate to limit the alternatives considered and also the ideological orientations considered to 3 or 4. Even if some politicians or other actors are not completely happy with the alternatives (ideological orientations) chosen in the study, the analysis will hopefully still be useful for them. A written PA document can still contribute to the illumination of the decision situation and is not the only input. And there is always the possibility to initiate a new complementary study.

It can be noted that the first version of Positional Analysis was presented in a PhD-thesis in 1973 (Söderbaum, 1973). The method has been presented at various places (for example Söderbaum 2000, 2008a). It has been discussed in relation to CBA, for example in a symposium at Roskilde University (Hanley et al, 2006; Costanza, 2006; Söderbaum, 2006). Other relevant articles have been published in *Journal of Economic Issues* (Söderbaum, 1987), *Ecological Economics* (Söderbaum, 2007) and *Journal of Environmental Monitoring* (Söderbaum, 2008b).

Elements of positional analysis

As already made clear, Positional Analysis, PA, is not a method in the sense that it starts with a decision problem and ends with a clear-cut (alleged) optimal solution. The purpose is rather to face various aspects of complexity and illuminate an issue for decision makers, such as politicians and for concerned actors. As previously mentioned PA has been described as a scheme of analysis at many places. I will here rather point in a desired direction (in the spirit of PA) for studies to be made in preparation for decisions. A number of questions may then be asked to judge or test whether a particular study is compatible with essential elements of PA:

- Is the study presented as a written document? (The questions that follow will be based upon an assumption that a written document is produced.)

- Is the historical background of the problem or decision situation presented in the document put forward to decision-makers?

- If there has been a debate or dialogue in newspapers or other arenas, is this debate with different opinions expressed, presented in the document put forward to decision-makers? How have the different actors perceived the problem and potential alternatives of choice?

- Has the analyst or decision-makers approached stakeholders and others concerned in an attempt to improve the understanding of options? Are the arguments of different actors made visible in the document put forward to decision-makers?

- Is more than one alternative presented for consideration and impact studies and does the total set of alternatives considered meet the criterion of many-sidedness in kind?

- Have alternative ideological orientations been articulated in the document and do these ideological orientations meet the criterion of many-sidedness?

- Is analysis of impacts multidimensional and disaggregated, reflecting a holistic conception of economics?

- Are various aspects of inertia (commitments, irreversibility, lock-in effects, path-dependence) and other long-term impacts discussed and made visible in the document? Is there a systematic attempt to illuminate how options at the first stage of decision-making will influence (limit or expand) options in future decision situations?

- If a decision mainly concerns some regional entity (local or national government); have impacts outside the regional entity been considered and made visible in the document?

- Is there any attempt to illuminate conflicts and commonality of interests in the study? Are significant equity issues involved?

- Are issues of ignorance, risk and uncertainty dealt with in the document and how?

- Have conditional conclusions been presented in the sense of relating alternatives considered to each ideological orientation in the form of ranking, for example?

- Are ways of monitoring actual future outcomes proposed in the study?

Depending upon the problem and decision situation faced, some questions are of course more important than others. There are also possibilities of choosing a simplified version of positional analysis as many have done. It is also clear that there are many possibilities to improve an information basis for decision making and also many possibilities to manipulate it. Among alternatives not only those that are close to each other in kind (for example house construction alternatives at the same place with only marginal difference in access roads) should be considered. And among ideological orientations, are there only varieties of market and economic growth orientations or is sustainable development part of the analysis?

Analysis then is understood as a learning process where some aspects of complexity are faced rather than assumed away. The issue of ideology and ideological orientation has to be faced rather than avoided. Various actors related to an issue or decision situation learn something that may be of value in future decision situations. The idea is also to strengthen democracy in a particular society rather than weaken it. Experts in the form of analysts have a role but so have all political economic persons affected or concerned.

A challenge to traditional accounting systems

Present accounting systems at the national and organizational level are closely connected with neoclassical economics. The main parameter in national accounting is Gross Domestic Product (GDP). Other macro-economic indicators are consumption, investments, exports, imports. These variables are all monetary in kind.

But as has (hopefully) been made clear, present threats to mankind are as much, if not more, of a non-monetary kind. Today "sustainable development" has become a key challenge where non-monetary accounting of a tentative or more standardized kind are very much needed. Few people among those who take part in the development dialogue consider GDP and GDP-growth to be a sufficient idea of welfare. Performance according to the UN sanctioned 17 "Sustainable Development Goals" has to be measured somehow for example.

In this situation attempts have been made to construct other one-dimensional indicators that reflect a more complex idea of welfare. I am sceptic to these efforts to construct indexes since they can easily be manipulated in different directions. A disaggregated approach is more promising even if such multi-dimensional performance measurement will never tell the whole story.

Present business accounting is similarly monetary in kind with indicators such as profits, assets and debts while many actors within and outside business corporations understand that more is needed. Also business and other organizations have to adapt to ideas about sustainable development. Corporate Social Responsibility (CSR) stands for such attempts to bring in ethical considerations in business management and decision-making. But a lot more is needed to "open-up" accounting practices (Brown, 2009; Brown and Dillard, 2015).

On the positive side, one can observe that there are some international journals in management and accounting where different ways of broadening accounting practices are discussed. I am thinking of *Business and Society*, *Critical Perspectives on Accounting* and *Accounting, Auditing and Accountability Journal*. Even more traditional journals such as *Journal of Management Studies* are part of this development. On the negative side we have to recognize the large number of professional accountants who have become accustomed to traditional accounting and therefore may have difficulties to depart from what can be understood as their vested interests. But even within the category of accountants there is presumably some heterogeneity (Söderbaum, 1991) suggesting that change is possible.

In conclusion then, new accounting systems need to be socially constructed:

- that respect the existence of more than one ideological orientation in a democratic society
- that observe the principle of disaggregation in economic analysis
- that take non-monetary impacts and "results" of business activities seriously (in addition to the monetary ones) and
- that illuminate issues of inertia in terms of non-monetary positional changes and impacts.

Understanding institutional change processes

Mainstream neoclassical economics is not a "revolutionary" discipline in relation to our present political economic system. It is rather a paradigm and ideology in defense of status quo. And in combination with neoliberalism as global ideology, neoclassical theory tends to contribute to an expansion of market forces, so called "marketization" to new fields and kinds of problems (Sandel, 2012). Market for pollution permits is just one example.

Institutions can be described in simplistic terms as rules of the game when actors relate to each other. There may be new laws but also voluntary systems of rules, such as standardization schemes. Environmental Management Systems, such as ISO 14 001, is one example.

Institutional change processes take place all the time and in different parts of the world. Individuals as actors perceive problems and opportunities for action in new ways. New ways of dealing with problems, such as standardization schemes, are articulated and applied by actors with similar experiences and in similar situations. Institutional change processes can be thought of in terms of "interpretation" (by some actors of specific phenomena, such as environmental impacts of business operations), "manifestation" (practical measures to implement the new rules of the game) and "legitimacy" (in the sense that the new rules of behavior are accepted by an increasing number of actors).

While modification of existing rules is important, one should not exclude possibilities of more radical change in institutional arrangements. Problems related to climate change chemical pollution and biodiversity loss are not under control and call for new thinking and values. In this situation, also some options for radical change need to be discussed seriously as a first step. Next chapter is a modest attempt in this direction.

CHAPTER 5
Politics for sustainable development

Economists, like other people, are political economic persons guided by their ideological orientation. We are eager to become accepted in some social groups. Just as political parties often are afraid of departing too much from one another, an economist may prefer a comfortable life by positioning herself close to other economists with respect to conceptual framework and ideology. Accepting the norms and standards of neoclassical economics is rewarding and constitutes a natural way of life. And since students are not exposed to any alternatives to neoclassical economics, the acceptance of neoclassical theory is not necessarily the result of a conscious choice. At some stage, however, a person may feel that she or he is locked into this theoretical perspective and category of economists.

"Critical thinking" within a discipline, and in the academy generally, is supposed to pave the way for improvements of a paradigm and even new theoretical perspectives. But critical thinking is not always appreciated. Supporters of neoclassical theory may feel threatened and call for "mainstreaming" of the discipline (as previously indicated for economics of biodiversity in the TEEB-study of 2010).

The pluralism strategy advocated in this book will make life easier for all of us. If economists understand that new thinking is part of our mission as economists and that values and ideology are always involved, then a degree of pluralism will more easily be accepted and even encouraged.

Today we are in a position where those who depart from the mainstream are no longer alone. There is a large number of associations, newsletters and journals for heterodox economists. Different schools of thought have their own journals, such as *Journal of Economic Issues*, *Review of Social Economy* and *Ecological Economics*. There are newer journals in English such as *Economic Thought*, *World Economic Review*, *Real-World Economics Review*, *International Journal of Pluralism and Economics Education* and in other languages. Books have been edited for example by Edward Fullbrook (2003, 2004, 2008) and Jack Reardon (2009).

In the previous chapters, I have tried to make clear that ideological orientation to some extent explains differences between paradigms and schools of thought. Some of us feel that the neoclassical paradigm is not enough to deal with "actually existing unsustainability" to use a phrase from John Barry (2012). As I see it, however, it is not the neoclassical paradigm that should be blamed but rather those who insist on a monopoly for this particular paradigm in introductory economics textbooks and more generally at university Departments of Economics. My belief and judgment after many years of participating in the debate about environmental and sustainability issues is that the neoclassical monopoly in combination with the dominance of neoliberalism explains essential parts of our failures in relation to sustainability politics.

A focus on perspectives rather than details and sub-optimization

I am supervising single students as part of an international Master course in "Sustainable Development" at Uppsala University and SLU, the agricultural university in Uppsala. In his Master thesis (2015) student Daniel Fior from Venezuela expressed his pessimism about present development trends at the national and global levels. He found some hope however in the writings of Donella Meadows (2015) dismissing large parts of environmental and development policies as being insufficient and too narrow. Referring to systems in all their complexity, Meadows discusses how they can be influenced and even manipulated. She uses a somewhat mechanistic term 'leverage point' and compares narrow and one-dimensional policies with ways of initiating change along many lines. Not unexpectedly she points to issues of paradigm or world view and power issues as more promising areas.

Meadows' discussion of leverage points is not far from our emphasis on perspectives in economics and with respect to ideology. Many are those who believe that mainstream economics, market ideology and the present political economic system can only play a positive role and will be conducive to deal with all kinds of problems. Reference is made to "Green Growth", "Green Economy", "sustainable growth" or similar terminology. Hopefully, something is achieved along these lines. But for me also perspectives at the levels of paradigm and ideology need to be explored and problematized. As economists we should not behave opportunistically by accepting mainstream economics and ideology. Our responsibilities include efforts to socially construct new perspectives in economics and to consider ideological orientations that challenge neoliberalism. While neoclassical economics and neoliberalism exist and should be taken seriously, it is also true that economics need be democratized.

We need for example to listen to radical voices such as the one of Richard Smith with the book *Green Capitalism. The God that Failed* (2016).

I suggest that attempts to contribute to new perspectives in economics for sustainability politics should be built upon the following premises:

- The *democracy* aspect has to be recognized implying for example that in a democratic society more than one ideological orientation is normally represented

- A related *pluralist perspective* implying that monopoly for one paradigm in economics education and research can no longer be accepted. Such a monopoly is contrary to normal ideas of democracy

- Having accepted that ideas about value-neutrality in economics are illusionary, *economists* like other actors in society should be *encouraged to participate in the development of ideologies and ideological orientations*, for example those that are compatible with specific versions of sustainable development.

I will start with the third premise, i.e. attempts to articulate the meaning of sustainable development. To do this, I need however to discuss some features of sustainability problems.

Non-degradation of the natural resource base

In broad terms sustainable development can be understood as non-degradation of the natural resource base in positional terms for present and future generations. This is close to the previously mentioned "overall goal" expressed in relation to the 16 objectives of Swedish environmental policy. Similar ideas about environmental and sustainability objectives have been expressed by many authors at many places. In the early 1980s, I suggested four "ecological imperatives for public policy" to be applied when planning and making decisions for a specific region. These ethical principles can be applied in specific decision situations concerning for example investments in infrastructure, such as roads, dams, energy systems:

- Alternatives with negative long-run impacts upon living conditions *within the region* should be avoided

- Alternatives with negative long-run impacts upon living conditions *in other regions* (and globally) should be avoided

precautionary principle

- Alternatives that involve *risks* of considerable negative long run impacts upon living conditions should be avoided (precautionary principle)
- If no alternative remains, research and development or other *search activities* should be initiated (Söderbaum, 1982).

At issue is however how to get there. Among alternatives considered in a case of dam construction none may meet objectives of non-degradation of the natural resource base locally, nationally and globally. In this situation one need to look for other kinds of alternatives of choice and therefore try to introduce new thinking and new values/ideology.

Thinking exclusively in monetary terms does not appear to be very helpful. I have referred to this as "monetary reductionism". Unfortunately, essential institutions in our present political economic system give priority to monetary or financial considerations. While such considerations probably will play some role also in the future, the main challenges these days tend to be of a non-monetary kind.

In the cultural climate which is largely the result of education and indoctrination in economics and neoliberal ideology, the kind of questions raised here may not be welcome. My position is however that since unsustainable trends continue, then also the present political economic system needs to be scrutinized.

Should monetary profits in business be regarded as an indicator of efficiency that reasonable people can be expected to accept? Here, I think we need a concept such as ideological orientation. For actors embracing neo-classical theory and ideology or neoliberalism, profits may be connected with efficiency. But if profits are increased by carrying over negative environmental impacts upon others and society at large, so called cost-shifting, or if business operations are out-sourced implying that people have to leave their employments, then there are certainly actors with ideological orientations where profits and financial outcomes play a different role. Profits may furthermore be the result of exploitation (in a monetary and non-monetary sense) of specific market actors, such as consumers, workers and taxpayers. There are more ideas of efficiency than one.

Minor institutional change happens all the time as previously discussed but it is probably wise to also consciously consider the design of major institutions in our societies. Are there alternatives to present institutional arrangements?

Candidates for institutional change

As an economist and political economic person, I may express opinions about single institutions and institutional arrangements globally, regionally, nationally and locally that have not adapted sufficiently well to sustainability criteria. When looking around it becomes clear that many of these institutions have been tailored or designed according to neoclassical theory that today appears incompatible with present challenges.

At the global level *The International Monetary Fund* (IMF) and *The World Bank* are major actors. As the names of these institutions indicate, they are defined in monetary and financial terms. Is this appropriate in relation to present challenges of climate change, biodiversity loss or chemical pollution? While there are signs that these institutions are using their authority for new purposes, taking climate change more seriously for example, also radical institutional change has to be considered.

Also, the *World Trade Organization* plays a major role in the present globalized economy. International trade agreements are encouraged, the idea being that so called "free trade" represents progress for all actors involved. Behind this are simplistic ideas based largely upon neoclassical theory. The recommendations exemplify technocratic tendencies in the application of neoclassical theory where the ideology built into the theory is not questioned. Contrary to such a simplistic view, it is here argued that in each trade relation between buyer and seller, many actors and interested parties are involved and they may differ with respect to situation, power position and ideological orientation. It can even be added that in each of the trading countries serious conflicts of interest between stakeholders are of relevance to study.

If there is a need for a global trade organization, then it should be built upon a different (multidimensional) idea of economics and upon sustainable development as the vision. The present negotiations between the EU and the USA concerning a so called TTIP agreement (Transatlantic Trade and Investment Partnership) does not respond to present problems but rather tends to aggravate them. The EU should, as I see it, reject this proposal as a result of tendencies in the USA of transnational corporations to influence US policies in their own interests. Proposal for an Investor-State-Dispute-Settlements institution suggests that normal ideas of democracy are side-stepped. This ISDS-mechanism would allow companies to sue governments if new government policies are expected to cause a loss in monetary profits for the companies.

Just as the EU has a democratic deficit, the same is true of the USA. But the EU and the USA are of course performing a bit better in democracy terms than nations with dictatorships that are also active in global trade. The *European Union* is broad in its activities but the priority of financial considerations in situations such as the EURO crisis in relation to Greece cannot be denied. The fact that those who originally came up with the idea of the EURO currency and of EU as a whole bear an essential part of responsibilities appears to be forgotten. Democracy in the form or referendum in Greece is not much respected.

Neoclassical economics and neoliberalism have contributed to further expansion of international trade. Increasing efficiency in the specific sense of reducing monetary costs for production and transportation of specific commodities has been the main goal. But this means that many non-monetary costs and impacts have been systematically overlooked. A single-minded call for "free trade" has been criticized by many (e.g. Dunkley, 2000). Let us recall arguments for "a greater measure of national sufficiency" as articulated by John Maynard Keynes:

> "I sympathise, therefore, with those who would minimize rather
> than those who would maximize, economic entanglement between
> nations. Ideas, knowledge, art, hospitality, travel – these are the
> things which should of their nature be international. But let goods
> be homespun wherever it is reasonably and conveniently possible;
> and above all, let finance be primarily national" (Keynes, 1933).

Just like the environment or the health of human beings should be protected through national policies, there are sometimes reasons for trade protectionism. An ideological orientation that takes sustainable development seriously will lead to a reconsideration of the free-trade versus protectionism issue. Local trade has many advantages. Ethical considerations as exemplified by the fair-trade movement can play a positive role and analysis should be multidimensional rather than one-dimensional.

Table 5.1 illustrates the implications of monetary performance as sorting mechanism. When considering single products (goods or services) or "commodities" as in neoclassical vocabulary, we can once more point to a distinction between monetary and non-monetary performance. A product – when it has been produced, transported and marketed in a particular way to its consumer or user and recycled or treated as waste – can according to specific monetary criteria (e.g. profits) be considered a success or failure. The product can similarly according to specific non-monetary criteria (e.g. ecological ones) be assessed as a success or failure. This leaves us with four combinations of monetary and non-monetary performance (Table 5.1).

Table 5.1 Products (commodities) can be assessed as successes or failures according to two separate sets of criteria i.e. monetary and non-monetary, for example "ecological" ones.

	Ecological success	Ecological failure
Monetary success	"i"	"j"
Monetary failure	"k"	"l"

In the present kind of capitalist political economic system some products are successful both in monetary and non-monetary terms (category "i" in Table 5.1). These products will appear on the market and since also non-monetary impacts are judged to be acceptable they do not represent problems. But there are also products which are non-monetary successes but fail in a monetary sense (category "k") and therefore are of little interest for business companies. In this case one can regret that the products do not appear on the market (or it can be considered for subsidies). Category "j" is of specific relevance in relation to sustainable development suggesting that there are products that are successful in monetary terms but fail seriously in non-monetary (e.g. ecological) terms. Governmental policies that reduce the number of "j" products and make "k" products move to the profitable category would improve the situation. Category "l" products are of less interest since they fail according to both sets of criteria and will not be produced. It should be added that this analysis is built on some idea that it is possible to aggregate within each category of monetary and non-monetary impacts meaningfully. To do this an actor with a specific ideological orientation is needed.

United Nations Environmental Programme (UNEP) and *United Nations Development Programme* (UNDP) are actors on the global scene who may refer to a vocabulary of Green investments and Green economy. But as in the case with TEEB 2010, they tend to play a mainstreaming role (Söderbaum, 2013; 2015a). Looking directly for the right compromise is not very rewarding. My scanty observations suggest that actors connected with these institutions never refer to heterodox paradigms. Normal imperatives of democracy imply that they also should illuminate alternatives at the level of paradigm and ideology.

Joint stock companies and business corporations, in particular the transnational ones, play a major role in our economies and societies. The existence of such companies is defined in monetary profitability terms. But the global economy – and parts of it – is mainly threatened by non-monetary problems. Does this mean that joint stock companies and business corporations are miss-constructed in relation to present challenges? Do we have to rethink laws related to organizations of different kinds? Minor adjustments through voluntary certification schemes referred to as ISO 14 001, Corporate Social Responsibility, the Global Compact are steps in the right direction that may open the door for new thinking in establishment circles and elsewhere, but are probably insufficient.

Banks are normally understood and assessed by shareholders in financial terms. This is certainly not enough in relation to economic performance understood in multidimensional terms. This brings us to the issue of global competition where success in terms of profits largely is a matter of reducing monetary costs in production. The easiest way of reducing costs in many companies is to reduce the labor force through robotics or to move production to other countries with lower salaries. Does this exemplify sustainable development? I feel that we have become locked into a system that does not function so well any longer.

The list of institutions to be scrutinized can certainly be expanded. Is the globalization trend of financial capital a problem in relation to sustainable development? Do national governments for example Ministers of Finance rely on a narrow and reductionist idea of economics? What about local governments?

The role of visionaries

Emphasis in this book is on democracy. Democracy means – among other things – that we should be ready to rethink some of our deeply held values that underpin behavior of various actors and present development trends. Listening to and learning from others is an important element in these attempts to look for a modified or radically changed ideological orientation.

Eva Kras, former President of the Canadian Society for Ecological Economics, argues that we, in particular, should listen to "visionaries" that have had a profound influence in the past and who also have a role in relation to present and future sustainability politics. In her book *The Blockage. Rethinking Organizational Principles for the 21st Century* (Kras, 2007), she points to a number of visionaries and their ideas that can be helpful in the present situation. Albert Einstein is one and Mahatma

Gandhi another. Among more recent persons she points to E. F. Schumacher with his book *Small is Beautiful. Economics as if People Mattered* (1974) and Hazel Henderson's *Paradigms in Progress. Life Beyond Economics* (1993).

I cannot here do justice to all the persons presented by Eva Kras. Instead I will only support her idea of the importance of visions and visionaries and point to my own list (which partly overlaps with the one by Kras). For me, Vandana Shiva is one with her many books, for example *Protect or Plunder. Understanding Intellectual Property Rights* (2001) and *Earth Democracy. Justice, Sustainability, and Peace* (2003). Other women who have been helpful in attempts to reconsider paradigms and ideological orientations are Noreena Hertz with her book *The Silent Takeover. Global Capitalism and the Death of Democracy* (2001) and Naomi Klein who has contributed to debate at a global level with *Fences and Windows* (2002) and the more recent *This Changes Everything. Capitalism vs. the Climate* (2014). In the latter book she scrutinizes tendencies of some environmental organizations in the USA to cooperate with business organizations in questionable ways. David Korten is my final example of a person who is helpful in our efforts to rethink the role of business in society: *When Corporations Rule the World* (2001) and *Agenda for a New Economy. From Phantom Wealth to Real Wealth* (2009) are two books that can be recommended to actors with an open mind.

I imagine that books of this kind, like some books written by heterodox economists, are considered controversial for actors who believe in neoclassical and neoliberal values. But if values and ideology cannot be avoided in economics and public debate, then it should be clear that we need to listen to voices from sources other than those that we are used to.

The responsibilities of economists and universities

Climate change, biodiversity loss, chemical pollution, land-use changes that threaten indigenous people are challenges of such magnitude that we all have reasons to reconsider thinking patterns and life-styles. It is not polite to only point to the responsibility of other actors or far away institutions like the WTO.

In relation to my own country, Sweden, I like to point to two examples of action needed. One is that Swedish governments over the years have chosen not to sign the ILO convention 169 about the rights of indigenous people. The Same population is relevant for Norway and Sweden but contrary to Norway my country tends to emphasize the rights to exploitation of land and natural resources, for mining purposes for example.

As discussed in Chapter 8 another Swedish responsibility refers to the Bank of Sweden Prize in Economic Sciences in Memory of Alfred Nobel. With few exceptions (Gunnar Myrdal being one and Herbert Simon another) this award has been managed to protect neoclassical economic theory. The professors in economics do not appear to understand Gunnar Myrdal's dictum that "values are always with us". We are back to arguments about the need for pluralism, democracy and for concepts built on recognition that there exists more than one value or ideological orientation in any society or community.

Business corporations can rightly be criticized but the same is true of universities. Just as we speak of Corporate Social Responsibility (CSR), we need to refer to University Social Responsibility (USR). Neither economics departments nor other university departments can hide behind an idea of value-neutrality. We all need to deal openly with value and ideological issues.

In the beginning of this chapter I referred to the political responsibility of individuals as economists. It was argued that it is easier to join the mainstream than to go "against the stream" to use a phrase from the title of a book by Gunnar Myrdal (1975). How can we take significant steps towards pluralism and paradigm coexistence?

CHAPTER 6

How students and other actors can contribute to sustainability economics and politics

The neoclassical perspective for sustainability politics focuses on markets. Markets, as well as market actors, are understood in mechanistic terms. It is possible for the state to regulate markets for specific commodities but the neoclassical ideology on the other hand informs us about the wonderful characteristics and functioning of the market, and that intervention with it should normally be avoided or minimized. In this sense it is a largely impotent paradigm and ideology for purposes of sustainability politics, protecting the *status quo* in terms of institutional arrangements and political economic system. Something more is needed in the present crisis situation, it appears.

Viewing the economy in mechanistic terms where the motives of consumers and firms are narrow and given, can hardly be seen as a constructive starting point for sustainability politics. Present unsustainable development should instead be seen as a challenge to the motives of many actors in the economy – and the political economic system more generally. Democracy in the title of this book points in the direction of individuals as actors, i.e. active participants in society and public debate with their ideological orientation and activities. We need to think in terms such as "political economic persons" and "political economic organizations".

In a democracy, politics starts with the individual as actor in all her roles: as citizen, family member, professional, consumer etc. The individual can behave in ways that facilitate the attainment of specific sustainable development goals (SDGs) or make the attainment of such goals more difficult. Acceptance of democracy, and the need to strengthen it, raises issues of responsibility and accountability which are totally absent from neoclassical theory. Assuming now that the SDGs are taken seriously in our society, it becomes relevant to inquire into the role of professors and students in academia. Later in this chapter we will focus on actors in other roles such as stakeholders and concerned citizens.

Actors appearing on different arenas with their agendas

Rather than the mechanistic view of sustainability economics and politics we have proposed a view of individuals and organizations as actors. They are political economic persons and political economic organizations guided by their ideological orientation or mission. An "actor perspective" is suggested with *actor*, *arena* and *agenda* as three key words. Who are the actors influencing economics and politics for sustainable development or the lack of such policies? What are their agendas[1] and in which arenas do they appear with attempts to influence future institutional arrangements and performance in sustainability terms?

When thinking of universities as arenas, the actors that first come to mind are university professors and students. Universities are institutions characterized by a certain division of labor. Each discipline is more or less integrated with other disciplines. Departments of economics may be quite isolated from other social science departments. There is a degree of protectionism centered upon the neoclassical paradigm. But neither economics professors nor their students are completely homogenous categories. Some professors/students are more open than others to pluralism and transdisciplinary work. This suggests that there are after all some openings for change.

What is the neoclassical position in relation to this idea of scrutinizing professors and students in relation to development concepts such as sustainable development? One tendency is to refer to positivism as a theory of science and the notion of value neutrality. Inquiring into the values and ideological orientation of professors then becomes a non-issue. It is believed or argued that science somehow stands outside politics – another case of division of labour.

But there are also tendencies to bring in more of the real world. Neoclassical "public choice theory" is such an attempt. Reference is made to "rent-seeking" behaviour of different groups in society. Farmers go together to increase their incomes in competition with other groups in society. Such explanatory theories have some relevance but when one looks carefully at farmers as an actor category, differences (and conflicting interests) may be observed. Some farmers are concerned about present unsustainable development and may identify themselves as "eco-farmers". The predictive value of crude assumptions about all farmers as one homogeneous category may then be questioned (Söderbaum, 1991). An "actor approach" as an alternative, recommends instead that one enters into a dialogue about ideological

---

[1] "Agenda" can be seen as the action part of "ideological orientation" or "mission".

orientation or mission with farmers as individuals and their representatives. "Rent-seeking" is not the only relevant objective at a time when an increasing number of citizens and politicians point to a need for values and ideological orientations of new kinds.[2]

Another metaphor frequently used in neoclassical theory is about "supply and demand". These terms normally refer to "commodities" traded in markets. Firms supply commodities demanded by consumers, for example. It is argued that monopoly is bad for consumers and society as a whole while a degree of competition will normally reduce prices for consumers, perhaps also improve quality and even lead to innovation in the sense of new commodities. In the university context, more precisely departments of economics, paradigms or theoretical perspectives may be thought of as "commodities" supplied by professors and demanded by students. At issue is the monopoly position of professors supplying only one commodity (paradigm) while students may demand more than one commodity and a degree of pluralism. Professors may need to do some market research to learn about the interests and ideological orientations of their students. The demand by actors other than students is another factor to consider (as well as the fact that some of us professors are not happy with the present situation).

How can students contribute?

There is a widespread belief that only established professors in economics can contribute to the advancement of economics as a discipline. Professors certainly have such a potential role. But when one realizes that ethics and ideology is involved in economics and that monopoly for one paradigm can hardly be regarded as compatible with democracy, it becomes clear that other actors with varying competences can also make a difference. Here I will focus mainly on young people who study economics at universities. They are normally old enough to vote in a democratic society. As professors we should listen to them as part of a dialogue.

How then can students contribute? One example is for students to get together in associations at each university and cooperate in international networks such as "International Student Initiative for Pluralism in Economics" (www.isipe.net/open-

---

[2] This is not to dismiss the ideas of rent-seeking behaviour altogether. I sometimes tend to connect the hypothesis of rent-seeking with the category of neoclassical professors in attempts to understand the tendency to protect the neoclassical monopoly at university departments of economics.

letter). Sixty economics student associations from 30 countries are now part of the initiative. Democracy, pluralism (with respect to theory and method), interdisciplinarity, the need for qualitative method (in addition to neoclassical emphasis on quantitative modelling), history of economic thought and economic history are key words in their argument.

Good arguments already exist and internet communication will make things more difficult for those who want to dismiss these arguments – but the power position of professors in the classroom situation suggests that change has to come from many quarters. Students finish their exams and leave for the job market while professors normally stay – with the possibility to continue just as before.

But some students continue to take an interest in the fate of economic science. A case in point is a book *The Econocracy. The perils of leaving economics to the experts* (Earle et al., 2017).[3] This book is written by three "dissident graduate students" and can be seen as being part of "a movement to open economics and reinvigorate democracy" to use the words by the authors (p. 24). At one point the authors refer to "the cleansing of economics departments" (p. 99) with the explanation that "non-neoclassical economists have been systematically excluded from economics departments across the UK" (p. 100). "Rediscovering liberal education" is the title of a chapter and attempts are made to present different schools of thought in economics and even ideas for curriculum review. It can be noted that Andrew Haldane, former chief economist at the Bank of England, has written a supportive foreword to the book.

Another book based on disappointment with the way introductory economics is taught at university departments of economics is Kate Raworth's *Doughnut Economics. 7 Ways to Think Like a 21st Century Economist* (2017). She refers to the history of economic thought and points to important steps in the evolution of what is now labelled neoclassical economics. The term used for her alternative "doughnut economics" may appear strange, but refers to the embeddedness of the economy in a socio-cultural and ecological realm. In her integrative effort she uses insights from ecological as well as feminist and institutional economics.

---

[3] Terms such as "econocracy" and "econocrats" when referring to technocratic aspects of economics are not new. The title of a book from 1975 by Peter Self, professor at London School of Economics and Political Science, is *Econocrats and the Policy Process. The Politics and Philosophy of Cost-Benefit Analysis.*

Arguments and pressure for change has to come from many actor categories, politicians included. Professors of economics who advocate or accept the calls for change need new associations, the World Economics Association (WEA) being one example and all "consumers" of economic thought need to become aware of the stakes in front of us.

Table 6.1 Roles of different actors in a university context

Role of...	Technocracy	Democracy
... professor	Preach mainstream neoclassical economics exclusively	Present mainstream and alternative schools of thought in economics. Encouraging questions and debate
... student	Accept the expertise of mainstream professors	Actor eager to learn and also form her own opinion
... media actors	Accept the expertise of mainstream professors. New developments in economics a non-issue	Interpret and interact with students/professors and other actors to improve functioning of the economy and strengthen democracy
... citizen	Accept the expertise of mainstream professors. Not expected to understand or take an interest in the manipulative aspects of economics	Learn about different views of economics. Actively participate in debate
... politician	Accept the expertise of mainstream professors. New developments in economics a non-issue	Interpret and interact with students/professors and other actors. Intervention considered in case of "democracy deficit"

Technocracy and democracy in a university context

The tensions between technocracy and democracy in a university context are illustrated in Table 6.1. Professors preach neoclassical economics and are essentially locked into this paradigm (left-hand column of Table 6.1). As part of the technocracy view, students accept the expertise of professors. Even journalists and other media actors tend to accept essentials of neoclassical theory and method and behave accordingly. The role of politicians is not much different. They may even hide behind the recommendations of representatives of science and deny or not understand the political aspects of science.

According to the democracy view of economics (right-hand side of Table 6.1), professors are more humble persons. Their expertise is of a different kind and any recommendation is conditional upon the perspective (theory and analysis) chosen. When it is understood that values and ideology are involved, the professor will respect the questions and comments by students in a new way. It is recognized that students have something to offer as part of a common learning process.

Students, media actors and politicians – in addition to their professional roles – are "political economic persons" with responsibilities and being accountable in the larger society. Students, for example, may agree with or disagree with the perspectives emphasized by professors and should be able to present their own positions (as long as they do not go against democracy itself).

Politicians will largely accept the relatively independent role of universities but need to intervene in cases where research and education in economics is based on an assumed monopoly for neoclassical (or some other) theory. It should be added that the calls for action by students have not been totally neglected by national governments. In Germany, the Ministry of Education and Research initiated a series of seminars 2003 at Deutsches Institut für Wirtschaftsforschung (DIW), Berlin. The seminars were focused on "sustainability economics" suggesting that something other than neoclassical environmental economics was needed. DIW can be described as a typical neoclassical research institute and considering the cognitive and emotional inertia involved, the impacts of the project are uncertain.

Similar efforts can be reported from France where a special study was commissioned by the national government. Two relatively open-minded neoclassical economists, Joseph Stiglitz and Amartya Sen, were the main individuals responsible for the "Report by the Commission on the Measurement of Economic Performance and Social Progress" (Stiglitz et al., 2009). Statistical issues of monetary measurement were emphasized, sustainability was discussed, but there are few signs that heterodox schools of thought were represented in the report. Although the immediate outcomes are limited, such initiatives are of course steps in the right direction. There are alternatives to the conceptual framework and language of neoclassical economics.

Qualitative studies with professors and students as actors

When students write a thesis as part of their exam, they have a chance to focus on some of the problems discussed here. As an example, I have supervised a student in a Masters program in "Sustainable Development" at Uppsala University who made a qualitative study of attitudes to pluralism of his professors at the university in France where he took his Bachelor degree in economics (Parrique, 2013). Those teaching economics are human beings with their own individual habits. They may focus on personal career development, where research and publications matter more than teaching. The latter activity easily becomes a necessary but secondary task. Some actors even admit that laziness is part of the picture when faced with a task of learning about alternatives to neoclassical theory or about the history of economic thought. It is, however, clear that students can make a difference by raising issues for debate. But a lot of inertia of different kinds is involved and pressure for change has to come from different sources.

Our emphasis on democracy suggests that students themselves should choose the subject matter for their own thesis. But a list of potential issues that can be considered may still be of value. A student, researcher or professor may investigate attitudes toward pluralism at a university department of economics by asking questions to professors and other members of the department of the following kind:

- Are you happy with the present situation of introductory courses in economics or are you in favour of some change? In the latter case: what kind of change?
- Are you part of teaching introductory economics courses and what is your role?
- Would strengthened pluralism in the sense of also presenting alternatives to mainstream neoclassical economics be a step forward?
- What kind of alternatives to neoclassical theory and method do you see as relevant?
- Do you agree with a statement that values and ideology is involved in introductory textbooks, teaching and doing research in economics?
- Will climate change and other challenges of unsustainable development be well handled within the scope of neoclassical theory and method?
- Is "democratizing economics" a relevant issue?

The interview should be carried out in a way that is open for discussion and be tape-recorded. It is suggested that each member of the department participating in the study is regarded as a political economic person and actor in a democratic society. Arguments put forward should be made visible in the study and professors as well as students be held responsible and accountable in relation to the immediate social context and larger society.

Investments in infrastructure: technocracy versus democracy in a public context

The tension between technocracy and democracy is not only relevant at the level of paradigm (as in Table 6.1) but also at the level of method. Our interest is about sustainability assessment where neoclassical Cost-Benefit Analysis, CBA, can be compared with Positional Analysis, PA, (Table 6.2). PA, as presented in Chapter 4, can be seen as part of an "institutional economics" paradigm.

Just as the neoclassical paradigm tends to attribute specific roles to actors in specific categories, the same holds for CBA as a method for sustainability assessment. As part of CBA the analyst becomes an expert in an extreme sense. The principles behind CBA inform us about correct market prices for purposes of aggregating impacts connected with each alternative. Other actor categories (such as stakeholder, citizen, politician) are expected to follow the recommendations about optimal alternative made by the CBA-analyst.

PA (right-hand column of Table 6.2) instead suggests a different set of roles to analyst, stakeholder, citizen and politician. As part of an actor perspective, where democracy is taken seriously, actors in all categories are encouraged to participate in dialogue and the problem-solving process. Stakeholders as well as citizens and politicians may point to relevant ideological orientations and alternatives of choice. Problem-solving in relation to investments in infrastructure or other kinds of programs or projects is regarded as a creative learning process where no source of new ideas should be excluded.

Normal principles of democracy tell us that the analyst, while knowing about PA as a method, should be a more humble person than the CBA-analyst. She/he should facilitate and document the process and make it visible and accountable for all actors involved or affected.

Table 6.2 Sustainability assessment. Role of different actors

	Technocracy (Neoclassical Cost–Benefit Analysis, CBA)	Democracy (Institutional economics, Positional Analysis, PA)
Role of analyst	"Expert" on correct market values and CBA method	"Facilitator", expert on PA method and dialogue. Conditional conclusions
Role of stakeholder	Essentially passive. Possibly asked about "willingness to pay"	Is encouraged to express opinions and take part in dialogue
Role of citizen	Silence will facilitate analysis and decision process	Is encouraged to express opinions and take part in dialogue
Role of politician	Expected to accept the authority of analyst and the result of analysis	Each politician decides (votes) on the basis of her ideological orientation and expected impacts of the alternatives considered

Source: Modified after Söderbaum, 2000, p. 84.

It should finally be made clear that the above attribution of relatively clear-cut roles to different actor categories necessarily represents simplification. In reality there is probably some heterogeneity in the category of CBA-analysts for example. While there is a need to study how actual CBA-analysts go about their task, it is here argued that there is a lot of truth in the statement that CBA as a method attributes specific roles to specific actor categories and that these roles are highly questionable in relation to normal (mainstream) ideas of democracy. PA on the other hand represents a step in the right direction.

CHAPTER 7

Ideology matters within and outside science and universities

The concepts of "ideology" and "ideological orientation" were introduced in Chapter 3. A broad definition of ideology in terms of "subjective perceptions (models, theories) all people possess to represent the world around them" by Douglass North was presented. Ideologies are "normative views of how the world should be organized" (North, 1990, p. 23). These writings by North however represent an exception. Mainstream neoclassical economists avoid such references to ideological concerns.

Why this focus on ideology and ideological orientation?

Why are concepts such as ideology and ideological orientation useful in economic analysis and governance? A first reason is that the term ideology is used in public debate about political issues. Politicians and political parties refer to their ideologies or perhaps something that can be described as ideological orientations. In Sweden, for example, there are tensions between the Social Democratic Party and the Left *and* three parties representing neoliberalism. It can thus be argued that economists who want their analysis to be relevant and useful for policy purposes should not avoid a terminology that is essential for politicians.

Mainstream neoclassical economic analysis is normally reductionist and often even one-dimensional in monetary terms, Cost-Benefit Analysis being one example. We have argued that analysis has to become multi-dimensional. Limiting oneself to a mathematical language is a questionable idea. Verbal language, visual representations and what is more generally referred to as qualitative elements must be part of analysis. There may still be a role for mathematical calculation, but only as partial analysis based on a single normative idea. But when broadening analysis a concept such as ideological orientation is needed.

Ideology, much like paradigm, is about perspectives and conflicts or tensions between ideological orientations and needs to be discussed openly in a democratic society. In relation to sustainable development such ideological conflicts are apparent. In Sweden, again, there are parties that take sustainable development seriously and those that prefer to downplay sustainability and discuss other things. In situations of ideological conflict, avoiding to illuminate such issues is a way of manipulating (consciously or unconsciously) a study.

Finally, broadening the language in economics is a way of getting closer to political science where the concepts of ideology and democracy play (or should play) essential roles. Actually, as we have argued, economics is another political science and the two disciplines focusing on management, governance and democracy need to be integrated in analysis of sustainability and other issues.

There is no single public interest

In its assumptions, neoclassical economics is essentially emphasizing the self-interest of individuals as consumers and shareholders, i.e. owners of firms or corporations. The economy is driven largely by such motives of individuals and the functioning of the economy is manifested in market transactions and economic growth in GDP terms. *neoclassical economics emphasizes the needs/wants of individuals and not communities*

The use of "ideology" can be regarded as an attempt to bring together motives and interests that concern the individual in a narrow sense with motives at a collective level. There are many kinds of collective categories, such as interest groups, political parties and citizens. The category of "citizens" can refer to those living in a local community, a national community or even the global community. Ideological orientation can also include elements other than human beings – such as ecosystems at various space levels.

Ethics is often thought of as a relationship between two individuals: "You should behave well in relation to your brother or sister." But there are ethical concerns beyond two-person relationships. Some economists, mainly in the heterodox economics tradition, refer to a public interest. Among ecological economists Herman Daly and John E. Cobb have written a book *For the Common Good. Redirecting the Economy Toward Community, the Environment and a Sustainable Future* (1989). The authors refer to the "common good" as if there was only one way of understanding the public interest. Neoclassical economists who emphasize self-interest tend to ridicule all kinds of references to a public interest. They see the relationship between self-interest and public interest in "either-or" terms. But the existence of collective or public concerns does not exclude self-interest. The two kinds of interest are here understood in "both-and" terms, and the words ideology and ideological orientation can be of help in bringing the two together.

Those who argue for consideration of broader interests often refer to "the" public interest (as in the mentioned book by Herman Daly). But our position is that human beings refer to many kinds of (what they see as) public interests in their ideological orientations. There is a diversity of ideological orientations among individuals related to an issue. And the ideological orientation of an individual furthermore varies between situations and over time. A learning process takes place where, for example, sustainability concerns may be increasingly internalized. While some changes in ideological orientation occur, an actor's ideological orientation is still characterized by some stability.

Ethics and responsibility is relevant at the level of individuals as actors. But it is also relevant and necessary to refer to a "collective responsibility". Individuals may downplay their own responsibility by pointing to their membership in some collective category of actors: "As a single actor among all economists I cannot do much to change the world."

Mainstream "neoliberal" business and market ideology

We have argued that there are many kinds of ideological orientation, and that identifying such ideological orientations and making them more visible and conscious to actors in society is a meaningful activity. When reference is made to neoliberalism as ideological orientation there is more than one way to describe this ideology now dominant in Western society. And a person like me, who regards the dominance of neoliberal ideology as part of the problems faced, will describe it differently from a person who embraces neoliberalism. But the fact that subjective judgments and preferences are present does not make the argument less interesting and relevant. We live in a democratic society where a dialogue between advocates of different ideological orientations is believed to lead to a better society in the sense that those who make decisions will know a bit better what they are doing. Dialogue, hopefully, also leads to a consciousness of the existence of different ideological tensions and options in front of us. Analysis of ideological options is not less important than analysis of impacts of given alternatives in a decision situation. We need to learn about the kind of futures various groups in society advocate and about ideas of how to get there.

Neoliberalism is an ideology where individuals are expected to emphasize self-interest and firms or corporations maximize monetary profits. Firms compete with each other in markets to lower the cost (and prices for the consumer) and improve quality, sometimes also supply new commodities as a result of innovation. In addition to efficient corporations the market mechanism is at the heart of the neoliberal belief system. And progress is very much connected with increase in income which implies increased freedom to buy additional commodities and consume. Neoliberal progress is also about attempts to increase the role of business by privatizing previously municipal or state-controlled activities and property, i.e. transferring them to corporations. These corporations may be national or transnational. Increased power of transnational corporations is not regarded as a problem. Progress for a nation is measured in terms of GDP growth, an aggregated indicator of the market transactions taking place in a nation during a year.

Belief in the extraordinary functioning of business and markets is such that advocates of neoliberal ideology are reluctant to accept state intervention of various kinds. There is a kind of belief in the wisdom of the market. It is admitted that market transactions may have negative impacts on third persons, so called "external impacts" but such impacts are systematically downplayed or disregarded. Still, such externalities often reduce the freedom of other actors to consume or meet their aspirations of other kinds.

Neoliberal ideology as described above is largely made legitimate by mainstream neoclassical economics. It can be argued that the conceptual framework and ideology of neoliberalism is close to the conceptual framework and ideology of neoclassical economics. And neoclassical economics, together with neoliberalism, works in the direction of strengthening the present political economic system and make it legitimate. This argument claims to be valid not only for the national economy but also the global economy.

Sustainable development as ideological orientation

There are of course many alternatives to neoliberalism as an ideological orientation. Since this book is about getting closer to sustainable development, I will focus on sustainability as alternative to neoliberalism. Again the interpretation of an ideology for sustainable development is subjective while leaning on parts of the contemporary scientific and political debate.

Sustainable development, as understood here, builds upon the UN sanctioned 17 Sustainable Development Goals (SDGs) listed in Chapter 2. This is a multidimensional view of development that clearly differs from the idea of economic growth in monetary terms. There is a focus on non-monetary impacts and on non-degradation of the natural resource base in particular (Cf. Chapter 5). Reference is also made to the need to improve (rather than degrade) the position of human resources and human beings in other respects, such as reduce inequality in a non-monetary as well as monetary sense.

Neoliberalism is largely based on a trade-off philosophy where all kinds of impacts can be traded against each other in monetary terms. This philosophy does not work well in relation to sustainability issues. In relation to the real world, the trade-off philosophy can even be regarded as a major mistake. Many non-monetary impacts are irreversible or difficult to reverse. Degradation of the natural resource base in positional terms is not something that can be easily compensated for in monetary terms. Rather, we should try to figure out and consider if and how non-monetary impacts will limit options in the future. Irreversibility is a central issue, not only in relation to climate change, but also for many land-use changes, pollution of agricultural land and water etc. Again, focus on estimated positional change in relevant non-monetary dimensions is our recommendation.

Given the present position of our political-economic system, no ideology can ignore the market. But what is needed is a different market ideology where exclusive reliance on self-interest is replaced by a focus on the responsibility and fairness of market actors. Political economic persons (PEP) and political economic organizations (PEO) replace neoclassical Economic Man and the profit-maximizing firm. Assumptions of PEP and PEO certainly do not exclude self-interest or other versions of narrow interests. This is something to be investigated rather than assumed as given. As I see it, we need some hope that market actors in the economy (and actors in other roles) sometimes bring in ethical concerns, for example, by attempting to behave in ways that are compatible with sustainable development.

As part of our sustainable development ideology and strategy, democracy is a primary concern while the market plays a secondary role. Rather than maximizing the private sphere as in neoliberalism, a public sphere including state intervention cannot be down-played as part of a sustainability ideology. A kind of ethical awakening in the private sphere has to go together with governmental reforms.

Even more fundamental kinds of institutional change need to be seriously considered at the national and global level. As mentioned in Chapter 5, the legal position of joint stock companies and transnational corporations need to be reconsidered as part of a serious sustainable development ideology. These issues need to be tackled also at levels such as the European Union and the United Nations. But in the present situation we cannot wait for others to act.

Sustainable development as ideological orientation suggests a need for a different paradigm than that of neoclassical theory. In this book a definition of economics as a discipline in terms of multidimensional analysis and democracy has been proposed. Reference can be made to "institutional ecological economics" where actors and institutions get a significant role. Institutions play a role in the present society and economy and institutional change of specific kinds influences the progress of an economy. But progress is not a neutral matter. It goes back to an actor's ideological orientation.

Relationships between economics paradigm, ideological orientation and political economic system

When faced with climate change and other sustainability issues, the mainstream economics paradigm and mainstream ideological orientation can be helpful in understanding problems and finding ways to tackle them (see the left-hand column of Table 7.1).

Table 7.1 Mainstream and alternative perspectives with respect to paradigm, ideology and institutional framework.

	Mainstream	Alternative
Paradigm	Neoclassical economics	Institutional ecological economics
Ideological orientation	Neoliberal ideology	Sustainable development as ideology
Institutional framework	Present political economic system	Institutional arrangements compatible with alternative paradigm and ideology

Neoclassical economics and neoliberal ideology have played a role in making the present political economic system legitimate. This system is not performing well in relation to the 17 United Nations Sustainable Development Indicators. If we wish to significantly improve sustainability performance we need to discuss alternative perspectives with respect to the paradigm in economics and ideological orientation.

Our emphasis on pluralism means that the neoclassical and neoliberal (close to) monopoly position is no longer acceptable. Research and education should focus increasingly on alternative perspectives to create space for alternative institutional arrangements.

CHAPTER 8

Conclusions on sustainability analysis and policy

How can the thoughts presented in this book be translated into constructive sustainability policy and action? The reader may get her/his own ideas from critically reading the above text, but here are my concluding comments.

Focus on paradigm and ideology

Many are those who, for different reasons, do not want to discuss issues at the level of perspectives and the behavioural and institutional changes that may follow. They prefer business as usual or *status quo* with dominance for neoclassical economics as paradigm, dominance of neoliberalism as ideology and a continued reliance on the present political economic system where only minimal changes are permitted. If these small changes go in the right direction then something is achieved. But the challenges in front of us are such that it would be a mistake to exclude alternatives at the level of perspectives.

University departments of economics have to move from neoclassical monopoly to pluralism. Alternative perspectives such as the ones advocated in this book have to be seriously considered in research and education. The threat to neoclassical hegemony will still be limited since we will – for some time – learn neoclassical economics to understand all those professors and professionals who have been indoctrinated in this particular way of thinking. Our advocacy of pluralism in economics furthermore means that paradigms may coexist rather than replace each other.

The dominance of an extreme market ideology in the form of neoliberalism need similarly be questioned. Behind neoliberalism is neoclassical economics and pluralism at the level of paradigms will presumably strengthen alternative ideological orientations, such as sustainable development, as discussed in previous chapters.

In the present society – and I am speaking of my own experiences from Sweden – there is a tendency to avoid open debate about paradigm and ideology in relation to the challenge of sustainable development. This means that the present dominant paradigm and ideology is protected. In this way the dominant political economic system is also made legitimate by dominant paradigm and dominant ideology (Cf. Figure 8.1). Too many politicians will continue to argue in terms of GDP growth, entrepreneurship, competitiveness, globalisation etc., as the (only) path to progress.

But Figure 8.1 also suggests that in a well-functioning democratic society, there are possibilities for change. There is a dynamic interaction between paradigm, ideology and political economic system. If dominant ideology, such as neoliberalism, is threatened then this may initiate change in what is considered as a relevant paradigm and perhaps also lead to changes of institutional arrangements such as political economic system. Change may also start in other parts of Figure 8.1 and have repercussions throughout the system of components.

Figure 8.1 Mutual interdependence between the dominant economics paradigm, dominant ideology and political economic system

Paradigm as conceptual framework and language

The word "paradigm" is often used with emphasis on explanatory models that have somehow been tested and accepted for further research and use. Neoclassical theory, for example, builds on positivism as a theory of science and focuses on finding optimal solutions and on prediction through mathematical modelling. For such purposes a conceptual framework is formed that is limited to mathematical language. The "paradigm" then stands for a closed logical system.

When I refer to the "institutional ecological economics" that has been presented in this book, the term "paradigm" instead refers to a "conceptual framework" that is more open but still claims usefulness when approaching a number of sustainability or other issues. This conceptual framework is a partly new language that claims to be helpful in understanding and constructively dealing with a set of problems in society. It starts with a new definition of economics emphasizing "multidimensional thinking" and analysis, as well as "democracy". "Actor", "political economic person", "ideological orientation", "political economic organization", "mission", "positional thinking", "inertia" are other parts of this conceptual framework and language that claims to represent a partly new way of looking upon the world around us – a new worldview.

The existence of inertia of different kinds has been a theme throughout this book. Cognitive and emotional inertia characterize the scientific community as well as actors in society at large. But when challenged, actors may reconsider their roles, thinking patterns and ideological orientations. Ideas connected with democracy are crucial when looking for new ways of dealing with problems. Visionaries and social movements can be of help in modifying or changing ideological orientations.

What we expect from different actor categories

Another theme in this book has been the idea that values and ideology are always present in research and education. Elements of subjectivity enter into the research process. This means that my own ideological orientation is not a secret hidden for the reader "behind a veil of value-neutrality". It should, instead, be openly declared. Also scholars as citizens and professionals are part of a democratic society. I will therefore point to some of my expectations of various actor categories as part of an assumption that sustainability issues are taken seriously.

What we expect from scientists, economists in particular

I am a professor emeritus with many years of experience of the functioning of university departments of economics and other social science disciplines, such as business management. As has already been made clear I consider the close-to-monopoly position of neoclassical theory at university departments of economics as a major problem in relation to aspirations of sustainable development. The two "facts" that (a) values are necessarily involved in research and education and (b) those employed at university departments of economics live in democratic societies – means that economics (in democratic societies) cannot be reduced to a centre of propaganda for those values that are built into the neoclassical paradigm. A degree of pluralism in education and research becomes the natural response. Value-neutrality is an illusion and there are many reasons to listen to the voices of students and other actors, politicians included, who understand that the present monopoly is dysfunctional for society at large. Professors of economics have no right to exclude competing theoretical perspectives connected with other ideological orientations, such as sustainable development.

Criteria when appointing professors and PhD-students have to be reconsidered, and institutions that support a continued monopoly for neoclassical economics have to be reorganized or eliminated. I am thinking of the "Bank of Sweden Prize in Economic Sciences in Memory of Alfred Nobel". With few exceptions this award has been given to neoclassical economists, many of them from Chicago University. It is difficult to understand the value of their contributions, but it is clear that the neoclassical monopoly is protected. A lot of prestige (cognitive and emotional commitments included) is behind the fact that the Swedish Academy of Sciences has not reconsidered or eliminated the award in spite of recurrent criticism.

Economics plays a central role when governing societies and nothing is wrong in rewarding economists for their scientific and ideological achievements. But economics was not mentioned in the will of Alfred Nobel and considering the unwillingness of leading mainstream economists to admit the ideological nature of their work, the prize in its present form is in my opinion a danger to society. The prize can however be renamed (excluding the reference to Alfred Nobel) and compared to other rewards where the role of ideology is recognized, for example, the Nobel Peace Prize or the Right Livelihood Award.

What we expect from politicians and political parties

Politicians and political parties have to take climate change and other sustainability issues seriously. Their agendas need to be upgraded with the possible inclusion of the 17 UN Sustainable Development Goals (SDGs). A focus on GDP growth can no longer be considered as sufficient. Many politicians and some political parties have understood that human survival on this planet is at issue, and that policies guided by neoclassical economics and neoliberalism have so far had a number of irreversible negative impacts on natural and human resources. But too many politicians tend to forget about inertia and irreversibility (influenced by neoclassical trade-off philosophy in monetary terms, I presume) and see these problems as not much different from other problems and issues.

In the case of Sweden, seven political parties have representatives in parliament. A power game is going on between three parties belonging to the "Green Left" and four political parties with more conservative aspirations. Each group or block of parties has difficulties in forming a majority for reasons of uncertainty about the aspirations of one of the more conservative political parties (which by the way lacks a credible program in relation to environmental issues). In this situation a coalition between parties to the left and some parties to the right is increasingly discussed. Considering the present programs of potential coalition partners, the prospects of sustainable development plans are not very bright. The parties in the middle still appear to be committed to a market and GDP-growth ideology, suggesting that these political parties have to take significant steps in a Green direction. This example only underlines that sustainability is a political issue and that politicians and political parties have to be taken on board in a dialogue and interactive process with many actors involved.

Dialogue within each actor category is essential as is dialogue between actors belonging to different actor categories. In addition to debate between politicians, politicians may engage in dialogue with economists, for example. But most politicians seem to believe in the positivist idea that scientists (economists included) are a neutral category of actors who should not be disturbed. The fact that economics is specific in ideological terms either is not understood or neglected. Hopefully, an increasing number of politicians will comprehend the ideological features of economics research and education. Economics as a discipline need to be democratized.

What we expect from local and national governments as well as the United Nations

With reference to neoclassical environmental economics, governments have implemented markets of pollution control to deal with CO_2 emissions – markets that essentially have failed. Politicians and actors in public agencies certainly understand that serious environmental problems exist, such as climate change, biodiversity loss and pollution of water systems – but the main idea seems to be to act slowly and that the neoliberal agenda as well as business interests should be protected. Too many politicians believe in a narrative where business corporations are worshipped for their contributions to GDP growth. A precautionary principle is applied but in a reversed sense. Business is protected rather than the environment.

Government regulations of other kinds (than markets for pollution permits) are certainly needed. Business corporations have to be regulated but also universities and their departments of economics should be encouraged to deal with sustainability issues in new ways. As discussed in Chapter 2 even the United Nations administration, such as United Nations Environmental Program (UNEP) and United Nations Development Program (UNDP) need to focus on alternatives to neoclassical theory. So far the willingness to learn appears limited.

What we expect from actors in the business community

The joint stock company is not well suited to deal with problems of a non-monetary kind. The single-minded focus on monetary profits – a kind of monetary reductionism – is sometimes innocent but too often affects specific actors (not being part of the market transactions), the environment and society at large negatively. As pointed out in Chapter 4, K. William Kapp refers to this systematic tendency of firms focusing on monetary profits thereby carrying over costs (of a monetary and non-monetary kind) on to other actors and society at large as "cost-shifting". It can be argued for example that oil-drilling corporations systematically transfer costs to others, ultimately the global population.

In newspapers we repeatedly read about corporations, often transnational ones, such as Exxon Mobil Corporation, Royal Dutch Shell, Rio Tinto, Gazprom, China Shenhua Energy, for their contributions to CO_2 emissions or about Monsanto for their behaviour in relation to small-scale farmers and risk-taking with pesticides and genetically modified organisms. The size and power position of such transnational corporations, even when compared with national governments, is of the sort that the joint stock company has to be questioned in relation to sustainable development among other issues. We have to encourage movements into other forms of organization, with missions that depart from exclusive focus on monetary profits. Firms in the financial sector deserve special attention.

The idea here is not to make general statements about all corporations or transnational organizations. While similarities may exist between organizations in one category, some remaining heterogeneity can also be observed. Each organization needs to be scrutinized and some organizations perform better than others in sustainability terms.

Business leaders and organizations certainly have roles in relation to other actor categories. There are thousands of lobbyists for example in Brussels or Washington DC who systematically try to influence government regulation to make life easier for their principals (and often more difficult for others). At issue is how these activities can be made compatible with democratic societies. In my opinion, the rules governing business activities need to be reconsidered at a fundamental level.

What we expect from organized social movements

"Organization" in neoclassical textbooks tends to be equal to "firm" or business organization focusing on monetary profits. Other organizations are not considered in analysis. And yet Civil Society Organizations (CSOs), often referred to as Non-Governmental Organizations (NGOs), play an essential role in our societies, not least in relation to sustainable development. Again such organizations will be judged differently depending on the observer's position and ideological orientation.

The legal status of civil society organizations is an issue to be considered. Personally, I support organizations like Greenpeace when they sue oil corporations and even the state of Norway for permissions of further oil-drilling in ecologically sensitive parts of northern Norway. But what about cooperation between CSOs, such as environmental organizations, and universities? When it is understood that value neutrality in economics is an illusion, professors in economics could very well also encourage studies that build on their interpretation of the mission of specific CSOs. The important thing is that value and ideological issues are dealt with openly in a democratic society.

What we expect from media actors

Actors in media play a key role as intermediaries between actors connected with other actor categories. They listen to many voices and hopefully not only (other) powerful actors. But the idea is not only to mirror the arguments of other actors. Media actors, much like actors in universities, are themselves members of a democratic society and have opinions and ideological orientations of their own. They may opportunistically (in the short run, at least) be silent about climate change, inequality or other issues, or they may deal with them openly and seriously.

Heterogeneity in each actor category

Neoclassical economics is very ambitious in the sense of aiming at explanations of how actors, such as consumers and firms, behave: "Consumers maximize utility within the scope of their (monetary) budget constraint", "Firms maximize (monetary) profits". There is also a theory, so-called "public choice theory", for the political behaviour of self-interested actors belonging to various categories. It is assumed that each actor category is homogenous with respect to interest and so called "rent-seeking" behaviour. The theory is applied to farmers, for example, and how they cooperate in politics to improve their incomes and wealth.

Again this theory can be of relevance in some situations. But the assumption of homogeneity in each identified actor category is a potential weakness. When observed carefully in reality the category of farmers can be subdivided into "conventional farmers" and "ecological farmers" with respect to cultivation techniques used and ideological orientation or mission. From a research point of view, further disaggregation is possible to smaller groups and down to each farmer with his or her particular resource position, ideological orientation and political behaviour.

I once visited a conference with the International Economic Association (IEA) in Athens under the leadership of Amartya Sen. Glenn Johnson, a U.S. agricultural economist, was responsible for a session on public choice theory and Johnson asked me if I was interested in contributing. I accepted and since I am a bit sceptical in relation to public choice theory I wrote a piece "Environmental and Agricultural Issues: What is the Alternative to Public Choice Theory?" (Söderbaum, 1991). I pointed to the fact that "ecological farmers" may cooperate just as "conventional farmers" are engaged in cooperation. Also, that it is more interesting and relevant to focus on the ideological orientation of different groups and single individuals and the power games that take place among farmers and scholars – as well as politicians. Cooperation exists across conventional actor categories, one may expect.

I think that an actor perspective or actor-network perspective, as indicated in this book, is more fruitful and also gives more hope for the future than the neoclassical public choice idea. The assumption that all farmers share the same interest (which then is expressed in neoclassical profit-maximizing terms) is a way of supporting mainstream or business-as-usual ideology.

In relation to firms or business corporations, we can try to make distinctions rather than group them all together under general statements about how they behave. Some companies have broader missions which are closer to the UN SDGs, others stick to the monetary and financial objective of profit maximization. In Sweden, for example, actors connected with the Federation of Swedish Industries (Svenskt Näringsliv) – that claims to represent all business corporations – do not show any sign of having grasped the ideas behind sustainable development. They furthermore appear to know nothing about alternatives to neoclassical theory. And still, some firms are more conscious than others about threats of climate change and other issues.

Strengthening democracy

As discussed in this book there is tension between dictatorship (and technocracy) and democracy in many places in the world. Some countries take steps towards more democracy, other countries seem to be part of a movement away from democracy and toward dictatorship these days. I hope that this latter change will be counteracted and reversed. We read about Turkey, for example, where many of those who do not share the ideas of the leadership are labelled terrorists and sent to prison. Journalists, even actors in universities, like professors, are jailed for reasons that appear arbitrary. And the legal system is rearranged to suit the new leadership.

Such series of events suggest that we need to continue the debate about the meaning of democracy. Democracy is about human rights – such as freedom of speech and freedom of organization. These and other human rights should be secured by a legal system which is independent from the actual political leadership. Democracy is, furthermore, about respecting the opinions and ideological orientations of others (as long as they do not go against democracy itself). Fair elections are not possible if leading actors in the government imprison members of political parties in opposition as has been the case in Turkey. Tensions and differences of ideological orientation should be regarded as normal and indeed constructive. Such tensions are part of problem-solving processes.

Single nations as well as groups of nations, such as the European Union or the United Nations face complex problems of various kinds. To deal with these complex problems it is presumably an advantage to listen to many voices rather than one single voice. Countries that are close to dictatorship can be expected to have special difficulties dealing with complex problems. They need to learn by listening to a dialogue that goes on in more open and democratic societies.

But democracy is, as we have argued, not only an issue at the level of nations and groups of nations. University departments of economics are one of many examples. The neoclassical monopoly suggests that countries like Sweden are not without problems.

In conclusion, democracy can be strengthened in many places and no country should be regarded as lost to dictatorship. In the present situation we need to work for democracy everywhere – including outside our own countries. United Nations is one of many platforms where this can be done.

New kinds of globalization

The term "globalization" is normally understood in neoclassical terms. It is part of the GDP-growth and market ideology where the competitiveness of firms in one country in relation to firms in other countries is a primary concern. A theory of "comparative advantage", although highly simplified in its assumptions is offered in support of the idea that "international trade is good" for exporting as well as importing countries while "protectionism is bad". A specific ideological orientation (among all possible ideological orientations in a democratic society) is necessarily behind such general statements about "free trade" and "protectionism". A little reflection will tell us that conflicts of interest are involved within the exporting as well as importing country. Countries that export commodities may suffer from polluting production facilities and importing countries (while purchasing at reduced prices) may suffer from loss of employment.

Globalization in a neoclassical sense is also about free capital markets and (although not advocated with the same enthusiasm) free labour markets. It is argued that financial capital as well as labour can move to new places to be used more efficiently. And the idea of efficiency is built on a specific neoclassical ideological orientation.

In the real world there are advantages as well as disadvantages of international trade. Free trade may be bad for some actors in specific situations with their ideological orientations and protectionism good. Actually, the 17 Sustainable Development Goals are largely about *protection* of ecosystems, land and water systems and the "global commons". Huge quantities of commodities are transported in containers between countries characterized by low-incomes (and thereby low monetary production costs) and high-income countries in different parts of the world. As a result of transportation in containers there is pollution in the form of CO_2, for example, with very likely irreversible impacts on climate. In what sense is this efficient and in what sense is this a sign of inefficiency and failure? Price signals, in this case monetary costs, to specific parties, too often give the wrong information in relation to sustainable development. There are non-monetary costs to consider in addition to monetary ones. We are back to the existence of different ideological orientations in a democratic society. There is no single efficiency idea that we all can agree about.

I would like to see that we all (professional economists included) increasingly think of globalization in terms other than neoclassical ones:

- Globalization of *democracy* as a set of ideas for governance

- Globalization of the *UN Sustainable Development Goals* (SDGs) as a set of ideas for governance.

The ideas of democracy have already been discussed as well as the SDGs. It is suggested that all actors in principle have responsibilities to participate and reconsider their behaviour and actions. The 17 SDGs in turn imply a broadening of ideological orientations and missions and represent a questioning of neoclassical simplifications discussed at various places in this book. Too many actors, myself included, have internalized too much of these simplifications and are now recommended to think one more time.

Strengthening democracy and emphasis on the 17 SDGs will furthermore make warfare within countries and between countries less popular. Efficiency concepts limited to destructive motives need certainly to be reconsidered in relation to different kinds of economic theory and to the 17 SDGs. This reference to ideological orientation (or mission) as a concept, will make us better understand what kind of efficiency idea we are referring to. The concept of ideological orientation also opens the door for the inclusion of equity or equality considerations – that few neoclassical economists bother about. To confirm my thesis about the relevance of focusing on "heterogeneity in each actor category" I like finally to invoke Joseph Stiglitz among neoclassical economists with his books *The price of inequality. How today's divided society endangers our future* (2012) and *The great divide. Unequal societies and what we can do about them* (2015). These studies may suffer from acceptance of some questionable neoclassical ideas but can still be recommended.

APPENDIX

A journey as an institutional ecological economist

Many people – including economists – get frustrated when they hear of distinctions between orthodox and heterodox economics and economists. They prefer to see economics as one thing. Communication is clearly facilitated if there is only one conceptual and theoretical framework. In many situations, orthodoxy represents a common conceptual framework for actors in different roles that will allow them to understand each other. But if our present global society faces problems of new kinds, then orthodox (or mainstream) economics may not be enough, and may indeed be part of the problems faced. The possibility that we need new languages for communication cannot be excluded. I am not in favor of simple explanations of the present environmental crisis (for example the threats of climate change) but I believe that the dominance of mainstream neoclassical economics has a role. Pluralism (rather than neoclassical monopoly) is very much needed.

The title of this book could very well be "Institutional Ecological Economics". As the author of this book and other books I consider myself as a "political economic person", i.e. an actor guided by an ideological orientation. I am listening to others and reading a lot, but I am not a neutral person in the sense often attributed to scientists.

For a long time, the two categories of mainstream, orthodox or neoclassical economists on the one hand, and heterodox economists on the other, lived separately with little communication taking place. It should be added that heterodox economists do not form one homogeneous category but rather consists of many schools as was indicated in the first chapter when referring to the study by Tanja von Egan-Krieger. She pointed in particular to feminist, institutional and ecological economists as three different schools. In recent times a dialogue has taken place among actors connected with different heterodox schools. Hopefully also some mainstream economists will understand that they cannot completely neglect heterodox ideas about economics.

Why are there different schools of thought in economics?

One positive example of a person who reflects upon developments within the mainstream and among heterodox scholars is Tony Lawson at Cambridge University. His book *Essays on the Nature and State of Modern Economics* (2015) can be seen as an attempt to scrutinize the mainstream as well as heterodox schools from an outside "third" position.

Tony Lawson is a specific political economic person with specific social and professional experiences, cognitive abilities and identity. He notes that many heterodox economists (but not all) are critical about the mathematical modelling practices among neoclassical economists and he himself supports this criticism. Lawson observes that there are mainstream economists (Colander et al., 2004) who argue that neoclassical economics is not static but that some new developments (such as varieties of game theory) are under way. Since the same authors return to a need for deductive mathematical modelling as criterion for projects to be accepted, Lawson expresses some skepticism in relation to the claims for newness.

More interesting for our purposes is Tony Lawson's judgement that heterodox criticism in terms of substance, for example focused on the present political economic system, is of less interest and relevance. It appears that Lawson here does not understand or neglects Myrdal's dictum that values are always present in our work as scholars. On page 147 in the mentioned book he cites a text by me where I suggest that the neoclassical conceptual framework with theories of the consumer, firms and markets ideologically is compatible with the present political economic system. In this way it is conservative and has little to offer in relation to recent developments in the real world with corporate social responsibility (CSR), fair trade certification etc. Lawson interprets my text as if I was arguing that neoclassical economists are – on purpose – working in defense of the present political economic system. I am not. I am rather contending that many neoclassical economists are unconscious about the implications of their roles and of the limits to their work.

On the positive side of Lawson's contribution is his acceptance of the concept "ideology" when discussing the achievements of various schools of thought. The insistence of neoclassical economists on mathematical modelling is referred to by Lawson as ideology. But this is still a narrow idea of how ideology can help us understand development and lack of development in economic science.

We can all speculate about the purposes of heterodox scholars as a broad category. My experience as a "political economic person" suggests that not only conceptual framework and theory, but also ideology is involved when an economist leaves the mainstream in favor of one or more heterodox schools. To make this credible I will exhibit fragments of my own story.

Early experiences as institutional economist

My university studies began with political science, statistics and economics in the early 1960s. I became employed at the Department of Economics, Uppsala University as a student adviser and later lecturer in international economics. This was a time when Paul Samuelson's *Economics* (1948) became popular in Sweden as an introductory textbook. Some actors employed at the Department became enthusiastic and a previous course in the history of economic ideas was considered superfluous and abandoned. Only the most recent ideas counted. The professor until then responsible for the mentioned course was asked to lecture on Samuelson's textbook or to leave the Department. I then witnessed the first academic power game in my career with articles in a local newspaper etc. The role and meaningfulness of mathematics and relationships between theory and the real world was part of the dispute.

The Head of Department, Professor Tord Palander, understood that I was not completely happy with narrow ideas of economics and the elimination of the course on the history of economic ideas. He suggested that I might find friends among institutional economists. I received a one-year fellowship to study abroad, more precisely in Lovain, Belgium. In a bookshop I came across a book with the title *Institutional Economics: Veblen, Commons and Mitchell Reconsidered* (Ayres et al. 1964). I found the book interesting and realized that Tord Palander's judgment of my inclinations were not completely wrong.

Upon my return from Belgium I became a teacher in marketing and consumer behavior at the newly established Department of Business Studies (later referred to as Department of Management Science), Uppsala University. This was a department more open in interdisciplinary terms and I felt more comfortable than at the Economics Department. As students at this department we learnt about alternative ideas about organizations by studying Herbert Simon's *Administrative Behavior* (1947) for example. Simon later received the Bank of Sweden Prize in Economic Sciences, one additional example of successful appointments of Award winners in the early periods of the Prize. I wrote my licentiate thesis "Profitability of Investments and Changes in Stock of Technical Knowledge" (1967) and my PhD-thesis on Positional Analysis (1973).

This was also a period when I became engaged in environmental issues. At the time of the Stockholm United Nations Conference on the Human Environment in 1972, I arranged a parallel seminar with Herman Daly, later respected as one of the leading ecological economists. I also became responsible for the environmental economics part of an introductory overview course in environmental management at Uppsala University. Interdisciplinary cooperation became popular and I lectured at the Departments of Psychology and Cultural Geography, Uppsala University.

I wrote regularly articles on environmental and development issues in a journal *Miljö och Framtid* (Environment and Future) from about 1976 until about 1992. Behind this journal was Miljöcentrum (Environment Centre), a foundation under the leadership of one of the leading environmentalists in Sweden, Björn Gillberg. This open engagement for various environmental issues, together with my call for new thinking in economics and agricultural policy etc. turned out to be a bit of a problem for my professional career.

In 1975, I was appointed "docent" in "environmental management and natural resource economics" at SLU, the Swedish University of Agricultural Sciences, Uppsala. I stayed there until 1995 when I moved (or was moved) to Mälardalen University, Västerås, and its School of Economics. For about 10 years until retirement 2005 I was responsible for an ecological economics graduate and later Master educational program at Mälardalen University. Many of our students were successful in their careers but there were also periods when environmental issues played a minor role in political agendas in Sweden and internationally.

In the 1980s, I was part of the US based Association for Evolutionary Economics (AfEE) and published in *Journal of Economic Issues*. The board of AfEE made efforts to internationalize the association beyond the USA and during a period I was a non-US member of the board. A similar association was initiated for Europe, European Association for Evolutionary Political Economy. I was part of it the first years but left when I understood that my ideas about institutional economics differed from those of Geoffrey Hodgson, an influential person in the association at the time. Differences of opinion (in present language "ideological orientation") are part of life in the academia and coexistence of theoretical perspectives may play a role even within the category of institutionalists. There is also an issue about where to spend your time and energy.

I was and I am a student of Gunnar Myrdal and for me the readiness to admit that values and ideology is involved in economics is a key issue. Gunnar Myrdal regarded himself as an institutional economist (Myrdal 1978) but was not totally happy with the views of members of the US association in this respect. I felt something similar in relation to the mentioned European association.

When I was employed at the Department of Economics, Uppsala University, early in the 1960s, I became the chairperson of an Economics Association (Nationalekonomiska föreningen) in Uppsala. I could then invite guests and not unexpectedly Gunnar Myrdal was invited. His book *Against the Stream. Critical Essays on Economics* (1972) played an important role for me. Somewhat later I was lucky to meet K. William Kapp when he visited Stockholm. Kapp can be described as the first environmental economist all categories with his book *The Social Cost of Private Enterprise* from 1950 which was later republished. I received reprints of articles from Kapp and I could follow the development of his ideas (see also Kapp, 2011). One observation is that Kapp and Myrdal were close to each other in approach and that they had friends not only in the German speaking part of the world but also for example in Japan. Among institutional environmental economists in Japan, Tokuei Shibata at Hitotsubashi University, Tokyo and Shigeto Tsuru have played a leading role, the latter author of two relevant books (Tsuru, 1993, 1999). Contacts with William Kapp go back to the UN conference in Stockholm 1972. This institutional tradition is today among others taken over by Masayuki Omori at Meiji University, Tokyo.

While being at SLU, I participated in international conferences with agricultural economists in Germany and internationally. As part of cooperation in agricultural economics between Nordic countries, I was together with Professor Kauko Hahtola at Helsinki University responsible for a PhD-course in institutional economics. In this period at SLU, I also began publishing in the *Journal of Interdisciplinary Economics.*

Two more observations from my time at SLU, Uppsala, are relevant for our discussion about orthodox and heterodox economics. In 1993 I published a book in Swedish *Ekologisk Ekonomi* and this book played a role in organizing education in environmental economics. Neoclassical and institutional approaches to environmental economics were presented as options in an introductory ten-week course. This was followed by a five-week course with either a neoclassical or an institutional approach and then a thesis which either could be supervised by neoclassical or institutional professors. Students were then "free to choose" in important respects which became, as I see it, a relatively successful arrangement.

At some stage the neoclassical economists and the leadership of the Department of Economics made the judgment that it is unwise to divide resources on two competing paradigms. A "critical mass" of neoclassical environmental economists was needed. I had to leave the department but was lucky in that a different university, Mälardalen University, was interested in my services. It should be added that the issue was not only about theoretical perspectives. Also ideology was involved. In relation to the mainstream at SLU, I was too engaged in environmental issues, I was too radical concerning agricultural policy advocating "ecological agriculture" and I criticized neoclassical economics.

The International Society for Ecological Economics

Neoclassical environmental economists had their international associations. But in the 1980s workshops were arranged in Stockholm and Barcelona with ecologists and economists invited. Ecologists were not totally happy with the efforts of neoclassical environmental economists and new forms of cooperation between the two disciplines were discussed.

In 1989, the International Society for Ecological Economics (ISEE) was formed and its first conference was arranged in Washington D.C. 1990 (Costanza ed. 1991). For me and many others, this represented a new opening and I have repeatedly published in *Ecological Economics*, i.e. the journal of ISEE. Later regional associations were formed, for example European Society for Ecological Economics, Canadian Society for Ecological Economics, Russian Society for Ecological Economics.

ISEE and our journal are not without problems. As in the case of the TEEB-study discussed in Chapter 2 of this book, there is a tension between new thinking often of a radical kind and those who call for "mainstreaming". Institutional factors such as the ranking of journals tend to push disciplines in a conservative direction. Mainstreaming essentially means compromise and that one returns to "Total Economic Value" in monetary terms or something similar.

We are then back to some of the key issues discussed in this book. Is it enough with one economics paradigm or should we respect and even encourage the emergence of competing paradigms? Is monopoly for one paradigm or pluralism preferable?

I have made my choice. The important thing is to understand that a scholar's preference for one paradigm is not only a scientific matter but also an issue of ideology. Since ideology is involved, compatibility with democracy becomes essential. And taking democracy seriously means that only pluralism is a defensible position.

Peter Söderbaum

Conclusions on democracy, pluralism and paradigm coexistence

I will end this Appendix by repeating the fact that "values are always with us" as argued by Gunnar Myrdal. As economists we may agree about ways of measurement in certain domains and refer to "truth" when pointing to the facts that follow. But when dealing with conceptual frameworks and theories in relation to development and environment we should probably accept more than one conceptual framework and more than one vision of the world, and even more than one "truth" if we want to use this word.

Referring to one single economics as the truth or being closest to the truth in theoretical terms is probably a mistake. Values and ideology are involved and have to be discussed openly. The existence of more than one perspective and conceptual framework then becomes strength rather than a weakness of economics as a science. And arguments in favor of one specific approach become less pretentious.

The fact that many economists only know of neoclassical theory and believe in it need not be our biggest problem. But the monopoly position (or close to monopoly position) of neoclassical theory at university departments of economics world-wide is a problem in relation to democracy, and represents, as I see it, a huge misallocation of resources. There is a miss-match between neoclassical advocacy for competition in commodity markets and their insistence on monopoly in their own profession.

I have presented fragments of my own story as economist but this story is just one among many similar stories. Just as we need to study cases to learn from decision-making and sustainability policy, it is probably profitable (mainly in a non-monetary sense) to study individuals as scholars and their career in terms of beliefs and professional positional changes. How do they look upon issues of inertia and opportunities for change in their own discipline?

Present development trends are unsustainable in many ways. All university departments have reasons to reconsider their responsibilities but economics, being expected to be one of the leading disciplines of governance and management, has a key role. A degree of pluralism seems to be a necessary step forward. I also hope that within the scope of such "paradigm coexistence", alternatives to neoclassical theory will get a more significant role, perhaps even become dominant.

Finally, the fact that economics is both science and politics means that politicians can express opinions about the state of affairs at university departments of economics and also should consider intervention as an option. We cannot leave it to the neoclassical economists themselves to decide what should happen to the present monopoly and lack of democracy.

REFERENCES

Ayres, C. E., Neil V. Chamberlain, Joseph Dorfman, R. A. Gordon, Simon Kuznets, 1964. *Institutional Economics: Veblen, Commons and Mitchell Reconsidered.* University of California Press, Berkeley.

Barry, John, 2012. *The Politics of Actually Existing Unsustainability. Human Flourishing in a Climate-Changed, Carbon-Constrained World.* Oxford University Press, Oxford.

Beckenbach, Frank and Walter Kahlenborn, eds, 2016. *New Perspectives for Environmental Policies Through Behavioral Economics.* Springer, Heidelberg.

Becker, Gary. S. 1976. *The Economics Approach to Human Behavior.* Chicago University Press, Chicago.

Becker, Gary S. 1981. *A Treatise on the Family.* Harvard University Press, Cambridge MA.

Biesecker, Adelheid and Sabine Hofmeister, 2006. *Die Neuerfindung des Ökonomischen: Ein (re-) productionstheoretischer Beitrag zur Social-ökologischen Forschung.* Oekom Verlag, München.

Biesecker, Adelheid and Stefan Kesting, 2003. *Mikroökonomik.* Oldenburg.

Boulding, Kenneth E., 1956. *The Image. Knowledge in Life and Society.* University of Michigan Press, Ann Arbor.

Brown, Judy, 2009. "Democracy, sustainability, dialogic accounting technologies: taking pluralism seriously," *Critical Perspectives on Accounting*, Vol. 20, pp. 312-342.

Brown, Judy and Jesse Dillard, 2015. "Dialogic Accountings for Stakeholders: On opening Up and Closing Down Participatory Governance," *Journal of Management Studies*, Vol. 52, No 7 (November), pp. 961-985.

Brown, Judy, Peter Söderbaum, Malgorzata Dereniowska, 2017. *Positional Analysis for Sustainable Development. Reconsidering Policy, Economics and Accounting*, (Routledge Studies in Ecological Economics 46). Routledge, London.

Colander, D., R.P. Holt, J.B. Junior Rossner, 2004. "The changing face of main-stream economics," *Review of Political Economy*, Vol. 16, No 4, pp. 485-500.

Costanza, Robert ed., 1991. *Ecological Economics. The Science and Management of Sustainability.* Columbia University Press, New York.

Costanza, Robert, 2006. "Thinking Broadly about Costs and Benefits in Ecological Management," *Integrated Environmental Assessment and Management*, Vol. 2, No 2, pp. 166-173.

Daly, Herman E., 1996. *Beyond Growth. The Economics of Sustainable Development.* Edward Elgar, Cheltenham.

Daly, Herman E., 2007. *Ecological Economics and Sustainable Development*. Edward Elgar, Cheltenham.

Daly, Herman E. and John E. Cobb, 1989. *For the Common Good. Redirecting the Economy Toward Community, the Environment and a Sustainable Future*. Beacon Press, Boston.

Daly, Herman E. and Joshua Farley, 2010. *Ecological Economics. Principles and Applications* (Second edition). Island Press, Washington D.C.

Dunkley, Graham, 2000. *The Free Trade Adventure. The WTO, the Uruguay Round and Globalism – A Critique*. Zed Books, London.

Earle, Joe, Cahal Moran and Zach Ward-Perkins, 2017. *The econocracy. The perils of leaving economics to the experts*. Manchester University Press.

Von Egan-Krieger, Tanja, 2014. *Die Illusion wertfreier Ökonomie. Eine Untersuchung der Normativität heterodoxer Theorien*. Campus Verlag, Frankfurt.

Engel, James F., David T. Kollat, Roger D. Blackwell, 1968. *Consumer Behavior*. Holt, Rinehart and Winston Inc., New York.

Fior, Daniel, 2015. *Toward Environmental and Social Sustainability: In Search of Leverage Points*. Master thesis in Sustainable Development, Department of Earth Sciences, Uppsala University (www.geo.uu.se).

Ford, David, editor, 1990. *Understanding Business Markets. Interaction, Relationships, Networks*. Academic Press, London.

Forsgren, Mats, Ulf Holm, Jan Johansson, 2005. *Managing the Embedded Multinational. A Business Network View*. Edward Elgar, Cheltenham.

Freeman, R. Edward, 1984. *Strategic Management. A Stakeholder Approach*. Pitman, London.

Freeman, R. Edward, J.S. Harrison, A.C. Wicks, B. L. Parmar and S. de Colle, 2010. *Stakeholder Theory: The State of the Art*. Cambridge University Press, Cambridge.

Fukuyama, Francis, 1992. *The End of History and the Last Man*. Hamish Hamilton, London.

Fullbrook, Edward, editor, 2003. *The crisis in economics. The post-autistic economics movement: the first 60 days*. Routledge, London.

Fullbrook, Edward, editor, 2004. *A guide to what's wrong with economics*. Anthem Press, London.

Fullbrook, Edward, editor, 2008. *Pluralist economics*. Zed Books, London.

Funtowisz, Silvio O. and Jerome R. Ravetz, 1991. "A New Scientific Methodology for Global Environmental Issues," In: Costanza, Robert editor *Ecological Economics. The Science and Management of Sustainability*, Chapter 10, pp. 137-152. Columbia University Press, New York.

Hampicke, Ulrich, 1992. *Ökologische Ökonomique. Individuum und Natur in der Neoklassik*. Westdeutscher Verlag, Wiesbaden.

Hampicke, Ulrich, 2001. "Grenzen der monetären Bewertung. Kosten-Nutzen-analyse und globales Klima." Pp. 151-179 in Frank Beckenbach et al. Eds *Jahrbuch Ökologische Ökonomik. Ökonomische Naturbewertung*. Metropolis, Marburg.

Håkansson, Håkan, David Ford, Lars-Erik Gadde, Ivan Snehota och Alexandra Waluszewski, 2009. *Business in Networks*. John Wiley, Chichester.

Hanley, Nick and Andrew R. Black, 2006. "Cost-Benefit Analysis and the Water Framework in Scotland," *Integrated Environmental Assessment and Management*, Vol. 2, No 2, pp. 156-165.

Henderson, Hazel, 1993. *Paradigms in Progress. Life Beyond Economics*. Kumarian Press, Bloomfield, Connecticut.

Hertz, Noreena, 2001. *The Silent Takeover. Global Capitalism and the Death of Democracy*. William Heinemann, London.

Hodgson, Geoffrey M., 1988. *Economics and Institutions. A Manifesto for Modern Institutional Economics*. Polity Press, Cambridge.

Hodgson, Geoffrey M., 2001. *How Economics Forgot History. The Problem of Historical Specificity in Social Science*. Routledge, London.

Howard, John A. 1963. *Marketing Management. Analysis and Planning*. Richard D. Irwin, Homewood, Illionois.

International Student Initiative for Pluralism in Economics. Available at: www.isipe.net/open-letter. Accessed 2017-09-21.

Jakubowski, Peter, 1999. *Demokratische Umweltpolitik. Eine institutionenöko-nomische Analyse umweltpolitische Zielfindung*. Peter Lang, Frankfurt am Main.

Jakubowski, Peter, 2000. "Political Economic Person contra Homo oeconomicus – Mit PEP zu mehr Nachhaltigkeit," *List Forum für Wirtschafts- und Finanzpolitk*, Band 26 (2000), Heft 4, pp. 299-310.

Kapp, K. William, 1971 (1950). *The Social Costs of Private Enterprise*. Schocken Books, New York.

Kapp, K. William, 1970. "Environmental Disruption: General Issues and Methodological Problems," *Social Science Information* (International Social Science Council), Vol. 4, No 9, pp. 15-32.

Kapp, K. William, 2011. *The Foundations of Institutional Economics* (Edited by Sebastian Berger and Rolf Steppacher). Routledge, London.

Keynes, John Maynard, 1933. "National Self-Sufficiency." *The Yale Review* (Summer). Accessed at www.panarchy.org/keynes/national.1933.html

Klein, Naomi, 2002. *Fences and Windows. Dispatches for the front lines of the globalization debate*. HarperCollins Publishers, London.

Klein, Naomi, 2014. *This Changes Everything. Capitalism vs. the Climate*. Allen Lane, London.

Korten, David C., 2001. *When Corporations Rule the World*. Kumarian Press, Bloomfield, Connecticut.

Korten David C., 2009. *Agenda for a New Economy. From Phantom Wealth to Real Wealth*. Berret-Koehler Publishers, San Francisco.

Kras, Eva, 2007. *The Blockage. Rethinking Organizational Principles for the 21st Century*. American Literary Press, Baltimore, Maryland.

Kuhn, Thomas S., 1970. *The Structure of Scientific Revolutions* (Second edition). University of Chicago Press, Chicago, Ill.

Kumar, Pushpam, editor, 2010. *The Economics of Ecosystems and Biodiversity. Ecological and Economic Foundations.* The TEEB study, United Nations Environmental Programme. Earthscan, London.

Lawson, Tony, 2015. *Essays on the Nature and State of Modern Economics.* Routledge, London.

MacKenzie, Iain, 1994. "Introduction. The arena of ideology," pp. 1-27 in Eccleshall, Robert, Vincent Geoghegan, Richard Jay, Michael Kenny, Iain MacKenzie, and Rick Wilford *Political Ideologies. An introduction* (Second Edition). Routledge, London.

Mankiw, N. Gregory and Mark P. Taylor, 2014. *Economics.* Cengage Learning EMEA, Andover, UK.

March, James G., 1994. *A Primer on Decision-Making. How Decisions Happen.* The Free Press, New York.

March James G. and Herbert A. Simon, 1958. *Organizations.* John Wiley & Sons, Inc. New York.

Meadows, Donella, 2015. "Leverage Points: Places to Intervene in a System." http://www.donellameadows.org/archives (Accessed August 4, 2015)

Mishan, Ezra J., 1971. *Cost-Benefit Analysis.* Allen & Unwin, London.

Mishan Ezra J., 1980. "How valid are economic valuation of allocative changes?" *Journal of Economic Issues*, Vol. 14, No 1, pp.143-161.

Myrdal, Gunnar, 1944. *An American Dilemma. The Negro Problem and Modern Democracy.* Harper & Bros, New York.

Myrdal, Gunnar, 1968. *Asian Drama. An Inquiry into the Poverty of Nations.* Twentieth Century Fund and Pantheon Books, New York.

Myrdal, Gunnar, 1975 (1972). *Against the Stream. Critical Essays on Economics.* Random House, New York.

Myrdal, Gunnar, 1978. "Institutional Economics." *Journal of Economic Issues*, Vol. 12, No 4, pp. 771-783.

Nolan, Peter, 2009. *Crossroads. The end of wild capitalism & the future of humanity.* Marshall Cavendish, London.

North, Douglass C. 1990. *Institutions, Institutional Change and Economic Performance.* Cambridge University Press, Cambridge.

Offer, Avner & Gabriel Söderberg, 2016. *The Nobel Factor. The Prize in Economics, Social Democracy, and the Market Turn.* Princeton University Press, Princeton.

Parrique, Timothée, 2013. *Economics Education for Sustainable Development: Institutional Barriers to Pluralism at the University of Versailles Saint-Quentin.* Master thesis in Sustainable Development, Number 136, Department of Earth Sciences, Uppsala University, Uppsala.

Pearce, David W., Anyl Markandya, Edward B. Barbier, 1989. *Blueprint for a Green Economy.* Earthscan, London.

Raworth, Kate, 2017. *Doughnut Economics. 7 ways to Think Like a 21st Century Economist.* Chelsea GreenPublishing, White River Junction, Vermont.

Reardon, Jack, 2009. *The Handbook of Pluralist Economics Education*. Routledge, London.

Rhenman, Eric, 1969. *Företaget och dess omvärld. Organisationsteori för långsiktsplanering* (The business corporation in its context. Organization theory for long-term planning). Bonniers, Stockholm.

Samuelson, Paul, 1948. *Economics*. McGraw-Hill, New York.

Sandel, Michael J., 2012. *What Money Can't Buy. The Moral Limits of Markets*. Farrar, Straus and Giroux, New York.

Schumacher, E. Friedrich, 1974. *Small is Beautiful. Economics as if People Mattered*. Abacus, London.

Self, Peter, 1975. *Econocrats and the Policy Process. The Politics and Philosophy of Cost-Benefit Analysis*. MacMillan, London.

Shiva, Vandana, 2001. *Protect or Plunder? Understanding Intellectual Property Rights*. Zed Books, London.

Shiva, Vandana, 2005. *Earth Democracy. Justice, Sustainability, and Peace*. Zed Books, London.

Simon, Herbert, 1947. *Administrative Behavior*. Macmillan, New York.

Smith, Richard, 2016. *Green Capitalism. The God that Failed*. World Economics Association (WEA) Book Series, Volume 5. Colllege Publications on behalf of WEA. Available at: worldeconomicsassociation.org

Spash, Clive L., 2011. "Terrible Economics, Ecosystems and Banking," *Environmental Values*, editorial, Vol. 20, pp. 141-145.

Spash, Clive L., 2013. "The shallow and the deep ecological economics movement?" *Ecological Economics*, Vol. 93, pp. 351-362.

Spash, Clive L. and Julie Aslaksen, 2015. "Re-establishing an ecological discourse in the policy debate over how to value ecosystems and biodiversity," *Journal of Environmental Mangement*, Vol.159, pp. 245-253.

Stiglitz, Joseph E., Amartya Sen and Jean-Paul Fitoussi, 2009. *Report by the Commisssion on the Measurement of Economic Performance and Social Progress*. Available at: www.stiglitz-sen-fitoussi.fr/documents/rapport_anglais.pdf

Stiglitz, Joseph E., 2012. *The price of inequality. How today's divided society endangers our future*. Norton New York.

Stiglitz, Joseph E., 2015. *The great divide. Unequal societies and what we can do about them*. Norton, New York.

Söderbaum, Peter, 1967. *Profitability of Investments and Changes in Stock of Technical Knowledge* (Licentiate thesis). Department of Business Studies, Uppsala University.

Söderbaum, Peter, 1973. *Positionsanalys vid beslutsfattande och planering. Ekonomisk analys på tvärvetenskaplig grund* (Positional Analysis for decision-making and planning. An interdisciplinary approach to economic analysis). Esselte Studium/Scandinavian University Books, Stockholm.

Söderbaum, Peter, 1982. "Ecological Imperatives for Public Policy." *Ceres. FAO Review on Agriculture and Development*, No 86 (Vol. 15, No 2, March-April), pp. 28-32.

Söderbaum, Peter, 1987. "Environmental Management: A Non-Traditional Approach," *Journal of Economic Issues*, Vol. 21, No 1, pp. 139-165.

Söderbaum, Peter, 1991. "Environmental and Agricultural Issues: What is the Alternative to Public Choice Theory?" Pp.24-42 in Partha Dasgupta ed. *Issues in Contemporary Economics, Volume 3. Policy and Development*. International Economic Association/Macmillan, London.

Söderbaum, Peter, 1993. *Ekologisk ekonomi. Miljö och utveckling i ny belysning* (Ecological Economics. A new Approach to Environment and Development). Studentlitteratur, Lund.

Söderbaum, Peter, 2000. *Ecological Economics. A Political Economics Approach to Environment and Development*. Earthscan, London.

Söderbaum, Peter, 2006. "Democracy and Sustainable Development – What is the alternative to Cost-Benefit Analysis?" *Integrated Environmental Assessment and Management* Vol. 2, No 2, pp. 182-190.

Söderbaum, Peter, 2007. "Issues of paradigm, ideology and democracy in sustainability assessment," *Ecological Economics* Vol. 60, No 3, pp. 613-626.

Söderbaum, Peter, 2008a. *Understanding Sustainability Economics. Towards Pluralism in Economics.* Earthscan, London.

Söderbaum, Peter, 2008b. "From mainstream 'environmental economics' to 'sustainability economics'," *Journal of Environmental Monitoring* (10th Anniversary Focus), Vol. 10, No 12 (December 2008), pp. 1467-1445.

Söderbaum, Peter and Judy Brown, 2010. "Democratizing economics. Pluralism as a path toward sustainability," *Annals of the New York Academy of Sciences* 1185, Ecological Economics Reviews, pp. 179-195. New York Academy of Sciences, New York.

Söderbaum, Peter, 2013. "Ecological Economics in relation to democracy, ideology and politics," *Ecological Economics*, Vol. 95, pp. 221-225.

Söderbaum, Peter, 2015. "Varieties of Ecological Economics: Do we need a more open and radical version of ecological economics?" *Ecological Economics*, Vol. 119 (November), pp. 420-423.

Söderbaum, Peter, 2016. "Behavioral Concepts as Part of a Participative Political Economics Perspective." In Beckenbach et al., eds, *New Perspectives for Environmental Policies Through Behavioral Economics*. Springer, Heidelberg.

Swedish Environmental Protection Agency, 2015. *Swedish environmental objectives* (www.miljomal.se/sv/Environmental-Objectives-Portal/ (Accessed Aug. 6, 2015)

Tool, Marc R. 2001. *The Discretionary Economy. A normative Theory of Political Economy*. Transaction Publishers, New Jersey.

Tsuro, Shigeto, 1993. *Institutional Economics Revisited.* Cambridge University Press, Cambridge.

Tsuro, Shigeto, 1999. *The Political Economy of the Environment. The Case of Japan*. Athlone Press, London.

United Nations, 2015. *The Millennium Development Goals Report 2015*. United Nations, New York.

United Nations, *Sustainable Development Goals, 2015*.

https://sustainabledevelopment.un.org (Accessed 2015-09-28)

Veblen, Thorstein, 1990 (1898). "Why is Economics not an Evolutionary Science?" Pp. 56-81 in Veblen, Thorstein *The Place of Science in Modern Civilization* (edited and introduced by Warren Samuels). Transaction Publishers, New Brunswick.

Wiemann, Joachim, 1995. *Umweltökonomik. Eine theorieorientierte Einfürung.* Springer, Heidelberg.

Wiemann, Joachim, 1999. "Die Methodik der Umweltökonomik". Pp. 17-51 in: Frank Beckenbach et al. Eds. *Jahrbuch Ökologische Ökonomie*, Metropolis, Marburg.

Williamson, Oliver E., 1975. *Markets and Hierarchies: Analysis and Antitrust Implications.* The Free Press, New York.

Made in the USA
Columbia, SC
28 February 2021